# ALFRED EDERSHEIM

## A JEWISH SCHOLAR
## FOR THE MORMON PROPHETS

# ALFRED EDERSHEIM

## A JEWISH SCHOLAR FOR THE MORMON PROPHETS

by Marianna Edwards Richardson

CFI

Springville, Utah

This is not an official publication of The Church of Jesus Christ of Latter-day Saints. The opinions and views expressed herein belong solely to the author and do not necessarily represent the opinions or views of Cedar Fort, Inc. Permission for the use of sources, graphics, and photos is also solely the responsibility of the author.

ISBN 13: 978-1-59955-112-8

Published by CFI, an imprint of Cedar Fort, Inc., 2373 W. 700 S., Springville, UT, 84663
Distributed by Cedar Fort, Inc., www.cedarfort.com

Cover design © 2008 by Lyle Mortimer
Edited by Annaliese B. Cox
Page design by Erin L. Seaward

Illustrations © 2008 by Jupiterimages Unlimited Corporation

Printed in the United States of America

10  9  8  7  6  5  4  3  2  1

Printed on acid-free paper

To my dear daughter, Sarah,
and my wonderful sister, Christine,
for their help in completing this book.

# CONTENTS

# Foreword

By David LeFevre,

*Fellow Edersheim Researcher and Author*

Like many Latter-day Saints, my first encounter with Alfred Edersheim was through James Talmage's book *Jesus the Christ.* I read that seminal work as a teenager, and when I saw Edersheim's *Life and Times of Jesus the Messiah* referenced in the footnotes, I scanned my family's small library for that volume. Disappointed in not finding it, I was then too busy with high school life to give it much additional thought.

Later, after my mission, I devoured Bruce R. McConkie's marvelous *Messiah* series, including the four-volume *The Mortal Messiah* books. There he quoted Edersheim even more extensively. Fortunately, by then the BYU Bookstore readily stocked *Life and Times*, and I acquired my copy. Though I read it with great anticipation, I got bogged down in the nineteenth century writing style and in the impatience of youth, laid it aside, though occasionally pulling it out to read particular sections over the next few years.

It wasn't until I made another serious study of the New Testament many years later that I reacquainted myself with Alfred Edersheim. Now his writing style, which had put me off all those years before, became more like poetry. I purchased his other books in print, including *Sketches of Jewish Social Life,* *The Temple,* and *Bible History: Old Testament,* each finding a place on my bookcase and in my personal studies. Each opened the world of the first century to me in new ways, complementing my learning from other sources and deepening my appreciation for the scriptures.

When Dr. Marianna Richardson first told me about her trip to China and her paper on Edersheim, I didn't know that her interest in the man and his work would pull me even further down that road. But her enthusiasm to share with others the value of Edersheim's wisdom and testimony was contagious, and we were soon working together, writing and researching his life and works.

With Marianna, I learned with fascination just how quoted he was in LDS writings about the scriptures—hundreds of quotes since the first one in 1903. I learned about and appreciated his life story, which I had never known, as we read his daughter's biographical sketch and as we found Professor Eugene Mayhew's more detailed life study in *The Michigan Theological Journal*. Edersheim's testimony of Christ was even more powerful once I understood how he gained it—and the price he paid for it.

I was thrilled to read his *Warburton Lectures* for the first time, sensing a passion in his speeches that went beyond the careful writing style he followed in his books. And I smiled and wept as I read his deeply personal autobiographical comments in *Tohu-va-Vohu*, his "notes to self" toward the end of his life. Through these efforts, Alfred Edersheim became a very real person to me, my own "learned friend" and companion in Bible study.

In this book you will discover Alfred Edersheim, the man and the scholar—perhaps for the first time, but certainly more deeply than before. Marianna's work here is the first time his life story has been fully told, the first time his writings have been topically examined across several books, and the first time his impact on the LDS community has been documented. Marianna has done a marvelous service to all those who love and appreciate the Bible and our Savior Jesus Christ.

I hope that this book will be a starting point for your journey as much as a destination. In other words, I hope that you, too, will come to appreciate Alfred Edersheim and desire to dive more deeply into his writings. His testimony of Christ rings true down through the years, and I echo Elder Bruce R. McConkie's hope that "Edersheim, and others who had faith and believed in the Messiah, according to the best light and knowledge they had, now that they are in the world of spirits where Elder Talmage continues his apostolic ministry, may have received added light and knowledge and will have pursued that strait and narrow course that will make them inheritors of the fulness of our Father's kingdom."[1]

David LeFevre,
June 2007

## NOTES

1. McConkie, *The Mortal Messiah*, 4:180.

# PREFACE

In the last few years, I have enjoyed my own personal journey discovering Alfred Edersheim. I was first introduced to his writings by Lynda Cherry and Marilyn Springgay. We were in a gospel study group together, and they started mentioning the works of Alfred Edersheim.

"Who is Edersheim?" I asked.

They looked at me quizzically. "Have you ever read *Jesus the Christ* by Elder James E. Talmage or *The Mortal Messiah* by Elder Bruce R. McConkie?"

I nodded my head, still wondering where this was going.

"Well, if you've read those books, then you have already read large parts of Edersheim's work."

They told me about their favorite chapter notes in *Jesus the Christ* and pointed out that they are quotes from Edersheim's works. They also explained that the long excerpts from *The Mortal Messiah* describing Jewish Sabbath day customs, the feast and festivals of the Jerusalem temple, the Bread of Life sermon, and the Last Supper are also citations from Edersheim. After hearing them laud his praises, I decided to get my own copy of some of his books. Once I read them, I was hooked.

Years later, I had the opportunity to present a paper at a Christian conference in China. I titled my paper "Alfred Edersheim: A Jewish Scholar for Christianity." During my study for this article, I found a copy of Edersheim's final book of random thoughts, entitled *Tohu–va–Vohu*. The beginning of the book included a short memoir about his life by his daughter Ella Edersheim. This gave me a lot of needed information about Edersheim the man. Following the presentation, one of the Chinese professors mentioned how the people in his country could learn from Edersheim's example of conversion. I think this professor's statement holds true for all of us. We can each learn something from his life and works.

Ironically, it wasn't until long after studying his works and life extensively, writing articles, and giving various presentations that I realized I was pronouncing his name incorrectly. I was presenting a lecture on Alfred Edersheim one evening when a friend of mine, who is fluent in German, came up to me after the presentation and graciously said, "I really enjoyed your lecture. Except . . . every time you pronounced his name you pronounced it incorrectly. It is not '*E*ddershime' with a short 'e' sound, but '*A*ders-hime' with a short 'a' sound at the front and no 'sh' sound." No matter how you pronounce his name, I know you will enjoy becoming more familiar with this great man and his works.

# ACKNOWLEDGMENTS

MANY PEOPLE HAVE HELPED me along my Edersheim excursion. My family has been a great support. They have had to listen to numerous outbursts, such as, "Oh, you have to listen to this!" or "Isn't this a *great* quote!" They continue to smile. Some have even become Edersheim "groupies" with me and have underlined copies of his works in their own libraries.

I especially appreciate my loving, caring husband, who supports me in whatever I do. He gives me wise advice and counsel, while helping me realize my dreams.

Dave LeFevre and Lynda Cherry are gospel scholars who have also been a part of this journey. Some sections of this book have been taken from unpublished manuscripts that we have written together. Dave especially did a lot of the research on LDS scholars' use of Edersheim. I appreciate their support of this and other projects.

A special thanks to Christine Thackeray, my sister, and Sarah Richardson, my daughter, who gave me the necessary help to finish this book.

ALFRED EDERSHEIM
(1825–1889). This is the only known photo-
graph of him, taken from his autobiographical
work *Tohu-va-Vohu*. Edersheim's passion for
Christianity combined with his Jewish heritage
make him a unique contributor to a greater
understanding of the Old and New Testaments.

# WHY EDERSHEIM?

THE QUESTION COULD BE asked, "What non-LDS scholar has most influenced LDS understanding of the scriptures?" And the answer could well be given, "Alfred Edersheim, a nineteenth century Anglican minister, a prolific writer, and a gifted linguist." His works have been studied and quoted in LDS-related publications hundreds of times[1] by a wide range of Church authorities and scholars over more than a hundred years. A portion of the most well-known of these works includes:

- *Jesus the Christ* by James E. Talmage
- *The Mortal Messiah* by Bruce R. McConkie
- *In Defense of the Faith and the Saints* by B. H. Roberts
- *Restoration of All Things* by Joseph Fielding Smith
- *On the Way to Immortality and Eternal Life* by J. Reuben Clark
- *Doctrine and Covenants Commentary* by Janne M. Sjodahl and Hyrum M. Smith
- *Gospel Symbolism* by Joseph Fielding McConkie
- *Latter-day Prophets and the Doctrine and Covenants* by Roy W. Doxey
- *Encyclopedia of Mormonism*, 4 vols., by Daniel H. Ludlow
- *Studies in Scripture* by Kent P. Jackson and Robert L. Millet

Although never introduced to the gospel in its fulness during his lifetime, Alfred Edersheim's concise explanations of prophecies and symbols in the Bible, together with his recognition of divine truth, add a "fuller and clearer"[2] witness of the gospel restoration in the context of ancient scripture. His insights strengthen and clarify the importance of consistent scripture study, the symbolic significance of temple worship throughout the ages, the direct fulfillment of prophecies concerning the Restoration, and the political and spiritual implications of the Savior's words and deeds within the framework of historic and modern revelation.

Jewish by birth, Edersheim used his knowledge of Jewish customs, language, and beliefs to heighten understanding of events and teachings in the Bible. After receiving a testimony of Jesus Christ, Edersheim's perspective on the Old Testament deepened, and he saw the unity of both the Old and New Testaments in their testimonies of the Savior. The two became one whole in design and execution, providing complementary evidence that Jesus was the Messiah for the entire world.

As a Christian Jew, he believed the Old Testament was the key to understanding the New Testament. Edersheim wrote, "We fail to grasp the sublime thought of the Old Testament. It is: Prophecy fulfilled in Christ."[3]

It was this fervent testimony coupled with his scholarship that fueled the strong influence he had in his day—and this combination makes his works relevant for us still.

Because of the many references to Edersheim's works, Latter-day Saints are often more aware of the content of his writings than of him as an individual. The following are some of the more familiar points in his writings:

- During the Passover feast Jewish homes set a place at their table and leave their doors open in anticipation of the return of the prophet Elijah.
- The shepherds who heard the chorus of angels declaring good tidings of great joy were actually Levitical priests who were watching over the sacrificial lambs for the temple.
- As a boy, Jesus went to the temple not for his bar mitzvah, but the year before, at the age of twelve, to observe the Passover rites at the temple for the first time.
- When the Savior announced himself as the Light of the World,

he was standing before the large and brightly lit menorahs of the temple during the Feast of Tabernacles.

The "hem" of the Savior's garment touched by the woman healed from an issue of blood can be more correctly translated as the "fringe" of his garment, referring to a prayer shawl worn by covenant Jews today.

The Savior declared himself as the Living Water during the water pouring ceremony of the Feast of Tabernacles in fulfillment of that long-celebrated rite.

The Lord's sacrament was instituted during the Passover Feast after the passing of the third cup, which is shared in remembrance of the blood of the lamb that had been spilt for them.

## JESUS PROCLAIMED HIMSELF
### the Light of the World in front of the temple's menorahs.

All of these concepts from Edersheim have been used in LDS writings. His perspectives have not only influenced the authors of these writings, but indirectly, his insights into Jewish traditions have guided many students of the Bible in linking ancient Jewish practices to their fulfillment in Jesus Christ.

Some would refute his scholarship and contemporary applicability because he wrote over a century ago, before gospel scholars enjoyed the source documents currently at their disposal, such as the Dead Sea Scrolls and first and second century Christian documents. It is perhaps true that some of his conclusions are superseded by these subsequent discoveries. But it is through the foundational understanding of Jewish culture and custom provided by Edersheim that those documents are best understood today. Edersheim's works also have a historical significance for the LDS community, as he was the first Jewish Christian scholar to be quoted extensively by LDS leaders and scholars.

For me, however, the deepest significance and beauty of Edersheim's writings is his testimony of Jesus Christ as the Messiah of the world and in his personal understanding of Jesus Christ as his Savior. As one comes to know Alfred Edersheim the man, greater spiritual insights emerge while reading his works. Because of his faith, he enjoyed true spiritual optimism in the midst of his trials. This optimism carried him through leaving his family and friends at the time of his conversion, and after committing to one faith, leaving everything again to try to follow greater truth in search of a "universal" or worldwide Christian church. Like the early Saints, he was persecuted for some of his beliefs and writings.

His writings often reflect his personal feelings as one who gave up all for his testimony of the Savior. In each of his most significant works, his preface includes a powerful assertion that Jesus is the Christ—which testimony drove his study and writings.

In *Sketches of Jewish Social Life*, written to bring the reader back in time to Christ's day, Edersheim wrote:

> Most earnestly then do I hope, that these pages may be found to cast some additional light on the New Testament, and that they will convey fresh evidence—to my mind of the strongest kind—and in a new direction, of the truth "of those things which are most surely believed among us." And now it only remains at the close of these investigations once more to express my own full and joyous belief in that grand truth to which all leads up—that "Christ is the end of the law for righteousness for everyone that believeth."[4]

Expecting possible criticism toward his views expressed in lectures and later published in *Prophecy and History in Relation to the Messiah: The Warburton Lectures for 1880–1884*, Edersheim wrote, "This only will I say, that within the conditions prescribed by this course, I have earnestly sought to set forth what I believe to be the truth of Revelation concerning Jesus the Messiah, as the fulfillment of Old Testament prophecy, and the hope of Israel in all ages."[5]

The introduction of Edersheim's exhaustive seven-volume *Bible History: Old Testament* states, "For properly understood, the Scripture is all full of Christ, and all intended to point to Christ as our only Saviour. It is not only the law, which is a schoolmaster unto Christ, not the types, which are shadows of Christ, nor yet the prophecies, which are predictions of Christ; but the whole Old Testament history is full of Christ."[6] These sentiments echo Nephi's feelings about the law: "Notwithstanding we believe in Christ, we keep the law of Moses, and look forward with steadfastness unto Christ, until the law shall be fulfilled. For, for this end was the law given . . . and we are made alive in Christ because of our faith" (2 Nephi 25:24–25).

In his significant book *The Temple: Its Ministry and Services*, Edersheim wrote, "At the close of these studies, I would say, with humble and heartfelt thankfulness, that step by step my Christian faith has only been strengthened by them, that, as I proceeded, the conviction has always been deepened that Christ is indeed 'the end of the Law for righteousness,' to Whom all the ordinances of the Old Testament had pointed."[7]

Finally, in the most quoted of Edersheim's works, *The Life and Times of Jesus the Messiah*, he stated: "And so, with great thankfulness for what service this book has been already allowed to perform, I would now send it forth on its new journey, with this as my most earnest hope and desire: that, in however humble a manner, it may be helpful for the fuller and clearer setting forth of the Life of Him Who is the Life of all our life."[8]

Edersheim's influence on LDS thought has been felt for over a hundred years. Elder B. H. Roberts first quoted Edersheim in 1903 after becoming acquainted with his works while living in England a few years before Edersheim's death.[9] Elder James E. Talmage used Edersheim as one of his major sources in writing *Jesus the Christ*.[10] President Joseph Fielding Smith quoted Edersheim in general conference on the centennial anniversary of the return of Elijah.[11] Finally, Elder Bruce R. McConkie nicknamed Edersheim "our learned friend"[12] because of his fervent testimony of the Messiah and his vast knowledge of the events surrounding Christ's mortal ministry.

In attempting to represent succinctly the thousands of pages of information and rich concepts that Alfred Edersheim has written, this book is divided into three distinct parts. Each part is based on a quote used by an LDS author in describing Edersheim or in referencing his writings:

- **Part 1—The Life of Alfred Edersheim:** *"The service of the Lord was the object in view"* is referenced by Elder James E. Talmage in his book *Jesus the Christ*.[13] This quote forcefully summarizes the focus of Edersheim's life. In order to understand the strength of Edersheim's testimony and the reason he influenced the heart and mind of LDS authors, we must first examine his life carefully.

- **Part 2—The Works of Alfred Edersheim:** *"So high an authority as Edersheim"* is a designation Elder B. H. Roberts gave Edersheim in the Church manual *The Seventy's Course in Theology.*[14] This part of the book is a concise discussion of the most fundamental concepts presented throughout his writings. Edersheim wrote from the Jewish point of view while explaining the traditions and beliefs of the Old Testament and the temple ceremonies. Yet his recognition of their fulfillment is centered on the divinity of Jesus Christ.

- **Part 3—The LDS Perspective:** *"Our learned friend"* is the appellation Elder Bruce R. McConkie gave to Edersheim in *The Mortal Messiah.*[15] In this section, each of the most influential LDS authors who referenced Edersheim are discussed. The ideas presented by these LDS authors often extend beyond his perspective and give us respect for the power of continuing revelation in helping us gain a clearer understanding of the Bible and the divine mission of Jesus Christ.

Whether this is a new journey for you in discovering this great scholar or you are simply extending an existing familiarity, you will enjoy reading the words of this fervent disciple of Christ. His powerful testimony of the Savior will strengthen your own faith in the mission of Jesus Christ the Messiah.

# NOTES

1. There are over three hundred Edersheim citations by various LDS authors on *Gospelink* (a trademark of Deseret Book). This is not a complete list of Edersheim citations by LDS authors since not all LDS authors are included on *Gospelink*, and some citations of Edersheim are not assigned to him, but to LDS authors who have quoted Edersheim.

2. Edersheim, *The Life and Times of Jesus the Messiah: New Updated Edition*, xix. Additional citations will reference this work as *Jesus the Messiah*. It is important to note that Edersheim did use Old English spellings (Saviour instead of Savior, fullfillment instead of fulfillment, defence instead of defense). Throughout this book, I have quoted Edersheim keeping his spelling differences.

3. Edersheim, *Tohu-va-Vohu [without form and void]: A collection of fragmentary thoughts and criticisms*, 112. Additional citations will reference

this work as *Tohu-va-Vohu*. The beginning of this book includes a memoir by Edersheim's daughter Ella.

4. Edersheim, *Sketches of Jewish Social Life: Updated Edition*, viii. Additional citations will reference this work as *Sketches*.

5. Edersheim, *Prophecy and History in Relation to the Messiah: The Warburton Lectures for 1880–1884*, xx. Additional citations will reference this work as *Lectures*.

6. Edersheim, *Bible History: Old Testament*, 8. Additional citations will reference this work as *Bible History*.

7. Edersheim, *The Temple: Its Ministry and Services: Updated Edition*, xii. Additional citations will reference this work as *The Temple*.

8. Edersheim, *Jesus the Messiah*, xix.

9. Roberts, *The Mormon Doctrine of Deity*, 179–81.

10. Talmage, *Jesus the Christ*, 160, 174, 188, 202, 281–82, 323, 341, 347, 391, 451, 504, 526, 573, 597–98, 599, 601, 619, 649.

11. Joseph Fielding Smith, in Conference Report, Apr. 1936, 74–75. Additional citations will reference Conference Report as CR.

12. McConkie, *The Mortal Messiah*, 4:22.

13. Talmage, *Jesus the Christ*, chapter 15, note 4. This is in reference to the Savior's comment: "The Sabbath was made for man and not man for the Sabbath." Talmage cited Edersheim's commentary on David's eating of the shewbread and why the priests forgave David.

14. Roberts, *Seventy's Courses in Theology*, 1:10.

15. McConkie, *The Mortal Messiah*, 4:22.

# PART ONE

# THE LIFE OF ALFRED EDERSHEIM

*"The service of the Lord was the object in view."*
—ELDER JAMES E. TALMAGE QUOTING EDERSHEIM

In order to understand the strength of Edersheim's testimony and the reason he influenced the heart and mind of LDS authors, we must first carefully examine his life.

# CHAPTER ONE

# LOOKING FORWARD TO THE COMING MESSIAH

THERE IS A STORY from the Talmud about the coming of the Messiah.[1] A rabbi dreamed that he met Elijah. He went up to the prophet with great reverence and awe to ask him a question, the question that was burning in his heart:

"When will the Messiah come?"

"Go ask the Messiah yourself," Elijah replied.

"Where do I ask him?"

"Go to the entrance of the city of Rome," he instructed.

"How shall I recognize him?" asked the rabbi.

"He is sitting among the lepers, tending their wounds, removing their old bandages and replacing them with new ones. The Messiah dresses each wound with tenderness following this procedure day after day. He does not want to disappoint the lepers or be distracted from his work. So, you must not divert his attention. In order to visit him, you must abide by these terms."

The rabbi agreed and went to the city gates to find the Messiah. The rabbi approached the Messiah, who was attending to the lepers just as Elijah had described. The Messiah acknowledged his presence, declaring peace upon the rabbi and his family. Then, the rabbi asked his question:

"When will you come, Master?" the rabbi asked.

"Today," answered the Messiah. He turned and spoke no more.

The rabbi puzzled over this meeting. Returning to Elijah, the rabbi told him what had happened. Elijah was encouraging. The Messiah had acknowledged his presence and pronounced peace upon him and his family. Because of this, the rabbi was assured a place in the world to come.

"He said he would come today. But he did not come," said the rabbi.

"Oh, Rabbi, he did not lie. The Messiah spoke the truth when he said today. He will come today—if only you hear his voice. That is the condition for his coming today. If only humanity would hear his voice," answered Elijah.

As a Jew, Edersheim had been taught stories like this since childhood. As a young man, he recognized and heard the voice of the Messiah as soon as he read the New Testament. For him, the Messiah came that day.

## HIS JEWISH BEGINNINGS

Born on March 7, 1825, in Vienna, Austria, Edersheim's Jewish ancestry was of "direct high-priestly descent."[2] His father, Marcus, was originally from Holland and a banker of some standing in Vienna. His mother, Stephanie, was from a wealthy Jewish family in Frankfurt, Germany. Both parents encouraged their children in intellectual and artistic pursuits, with German, French, and English all spoken in the home. Being raised in a multilingual home would have a keen influence on his later life and career.

Alfred was the youngest of their four children. He was unusually precocious and started his grammar school education with a resident tutor. At the age of ten, he entered a gymnasium. The Austrian gymnasiums were private preparatory schools for boys preparing for a university education. Illustrating his keen intelligence and social amiability, Alfred became the first Jewish boy to receive an academic award from the gymnasium he attended. He was also a high-spirited young man who enjoyed teenage fun. Once, he was arrested for mimicking the sentinels on duty. He was only released when the police discovered who his father was. His physical appearance as a youth is described as "slight, alert, . . . clad in white breeches and black velveteen coat, with long fair curls lying on his shoulders."[3]

## THE POPULATION OF
Vienna, Austria, was
317,768 in 1830

While studying at the gymnasium, he also attended the Jewish school connected to the local synagogue where he was taught the cultural and spiritual traditions of his people.[4] He learned Hebrew, Jewish history and culture, and received a thorough introduction to the Jewish Bible—the Old Testament—and its teachings. The teachings of his youth became the basis for his faith in Jehovah and love of the scriptures.

## THE AUSTRIAN GYMNASIUMS
were private preparatory schools for boys preparing for a university education. Illustrating his keen intelligence and social amiability, Alfred became the first Jewish boy to receive an academic award from the gymnasium he attended.

*16 yrs*

In 1841, he continued his studies at the University of Vienna in philosophy with a personal interest in literature. In his first semester at the university, he started a literary club and was very active in student debates. Just after his first exams, Alfred's father experienced a devastating financial reversal. Dutch correspondents caused the collapse of his father's bank. Edersheim's parents lost everything, and he had to leave the university before he could finish his degree.

This was a very difficult time for young Alfred. While his parents were trying to recover financially, Alfred did not want to be a burden to his parents. His future looked bleak. As the youngest son in a Jewish family, he had few prospects. In 1845, with only "a few dollars in his pocket,"[5] he followed two of his tutors to Pest, Hungary (modern Budapest), a city of greater hope and more freedom for Jews. He continued his studies at the University of Pest, but he was now paying his own way through school. He hoped to work as a teacher of languages, since he was already fluent or literate in at least five,[6] and to continue his university studies in literature and writing.

## DISCOVERING THE NEW TESTAMENT

In his pursuit of employment, Edersheim was introduced to Dr. John Duncan, a Presbyterian chaplain from Scotland, and his two young colleagues, Mr. Wingate and Mr. Smith.[7] They had been chaplains to Scottish workers building a suspension bridge over the Danube River. They were trying to start a Christian mission among the Jews in Hungary. The missionaries employed young Edersheim as a German tutor and translator.

Having been raised in a home of privilege, Alfred was impressed by the simple, holy life these men led, and they soon became friends. Their friendship led to these missionaries presenting young Alfred with the message of the New Testament. Edersheim wrote:

> I had never seen a New Testament till I received the first copy from the hands of the Presbyterian ministers. I shall never forget the first impression of "The Sermon on the Mount," nor yet the surprise, and deep feeling, by which the reading of the New Testament followed. That which I had so hated was not Christianity; that which I had not known, and which opened such untold depths, was the teaching of Jesus of Nazareth. I became a Christian, and was baptized by the pastor of the Reformed Church at Pesth.[8]

His feelings were now different about Christianity and the New Testament. He had been taught that these things were unholy, unclean, and even things to be hated. The teachings of the Sermon on the Mount had changed him as they had the people who originally heard Jesus' teachings: "When Jesus had ended these sayings, the people were astonished at his doctrine for he taught them as one having authority" (Matthew 7:28–29). Edersheim was astonished by the doctrine he heard and read, for they were dissimilar to what he had been taught while a young boy in the synagogue.

But his testimony of the Old Testament did not change. It only broadened and deepened as he looked at the Old Testament through New Testament eyes: "There is unity, continuity, and progress in the teaching of the Old Testament and that all in it is prophetic of the Christ."[9] He felt Christianity gave him a greater understanding of the traditions and history of the Old Testament, which he had been taught since his youth. His new faith gave his old faith form and purpose.

Later in his life, Edersheim reflected upon his conversion to Christianity in his personal journal: "I can say a great many things in favour of the Lord Jesus Christ—of His Power, Grace, and Love. But the greatest I can say of them is: that He has received me. Thus, the faith of the poorest sinner brings the greatest glory to Christ."[10]

His conversion would take a lifetime of testing and trials. After he was converted, he would try to strengthen his brethren (Luke 22:32) by becoming a preacher, a missionary, and a writer of spiritual insights on the Old and New Testament.

# NOTES

1. Bleefeld and Shook, *Saving the World Entire*, 223–24 (Talmud source: *Sanhedrin* 98a).
2. Edersheim, *Tohu-va-Vohu*, vi. Very little has been formally written on the life of Alfred Edersheim. The most definitive work is a memoir written by Alfred Edersheim's daughter Ella preceding his own thoughts in the book. A more recent work is a biography written by Dr. George Mayhew in the *Michigan Theological Journal* entitled "Alfred Edersheim—A Brief Biography" (see bibliography).
3. Edersheim, *Tohu-va-Vohu*, x.
4. Driver and Agnew, "Alfred Edersheim," 696.
5. Edersheim, *Tohu-va-Vohu*, x.
6. Besides the German, French, and English he learned at home, he had studied Hebrew at the Jewish school and Latin at the university; *Tohu-va-Vohu*, xiii. Mayhew believes he also knew Greek and Dutch by this time, which would make seven, a remarkable number for anyone, but especially for a young university student. See Mayhew, "Alfred Edersheim," 171.
7. Blaikie and Matthew, "John Duncan," 239.
8. Edersheim, *Tohu-va-Vohu*, xiii.
9. Edersheim, *Lectures*, 3.
10. Edersheim, *Tohu-va-Vohu*, 20.

# CHAPTER TWO

# HIS BIRTH FROM ABOVE

BECAUSE OF HIS DECISION to accept Christ, Edersheim's life was completely altered. The change in his inner life had a corresponding effect on his outer decisions. He replaced his studies in literature with theology, with the final goal of entering the ministry and sharing his strong testimony. His willingness to change his course in search of truth and service is what brought about this "birth from above."[1] However, he was not yet acquainted with the various divisions of Christian churches. He explained, "Of 'Church questions' I knew absolutely nothing. They did not as yet arise. I had only learned the doctrines of Christianity from the New Testament, and the only outward church I really knew . . . was that of my teachers, the Scottish ministers."[2] He was immediately baptized into the Church of Scotland, unaware of the differences between Christian sects but having a firm testimony in Jesus Christ and the Bible.

THE EDINBURGH LIBRARY was probably a place young Edersheim frequented while studying at New College.

Wanting to learn more, he followed his missionary friends to their homeland in Edinburgh. Under Dr. John Duncan's tutelage, Alfred began to read and study about his newfound religion. He entered the New College of Edinburgh, Scotland, where Dr. Duncan was the Chair of Oriental Languages. In 1843, at the age of eighteen, Alfred Edersheim entered the New College of Edinburgh to study Latin, Greek, Hebrew, Logic, History, and Moral Philosophy. [3]

## A NEW TEACHER AND NEW MAN

In the summer of 1844, Alfred Edersheim went to the University of Berlin as a visiting scholar to do additional research on Christian philosophy and biblical studies. A notable professor in Berlin under whom Alfred studied was Johann August Wilhelm Neander (1789–1850). He had also been born a Jew and converted to Christianity when he was seventeen years old, the same age as Edersheim at his conversion. At baptism, he changed his last name to Neander, which means *new man*,[4] as a symbol of his spiritual rebirth.

At the time of their meeting, Professor Neander, who was in his fifties, was an accomplished author and intense scholar of the early Christian church. Neander felt that the gospel of Jesus Christ could stand up to the most exhaustive inspection: "Nothing but what can stand as truth before the scrutiny of genuine science, of a science which does not see through the glass of a particular philosophical or dogmatic school, can be profitable for instruction, doctrine, and reproof."[5] These feelings about spiritual truth withstanding the examination of science are similar to thoughts Edersheim expressed later in his life during his Warburton Lecture Series when he said, "For the end is certain—not that full and free criticism may be suppressed, but that it may be utilized, that so on the evening of the battle there may be assured peace, and the golden light shine around the old truth in her new garments of conquest, revealing the full perfection of her beauty."[6] This fearless enthusiasm to search out truth without bending to established dogma allowed Edersheim to unfold gospel truths lost to many other Bible scholars of his day.

Although we do not have an autobiography of Edersheim's life, through his journal writings we can catch a glimpse of his feelings and perspectives. His subsequent scriptural commentaries are

often intensely personal, reflecting his rejoicing heart, enlightened eyes, and missionary zeal in sharing spiritual insights with others. Rather than writing to a distant third person, he often bore an intimate testimony encouraging readers to rededicate themselves to follow Christ. His writings would often start out being very analytical; but then, a personal "I" or "we" comment would be interspersed in the text to emphasize what the reader's own feelings should be about the scripture story or to express his testimony on a gospel principle.

He especially expressed tender feelings about conversion stories to Christianity, reflecting an obvious kinship with the early Jewish Christians who had to establish new religious traditions and beliefs, as he and Neander had. Particularly, Nicodemus's visits to the Savior and his questions on being born again were personally meaningful for Edersheim. His commentary on this story gives greater insight into his feelings about what it means to be truly converted to the gospel of Jesus Christ.

## NICODEMUS CONCLUDED THAT
Jesus was a teacher come from God.
"The submission of heart, mind, and life to
Him as our Divine King . . . can only be
learned from Christ."—Alfred Edersheim

## THE EXAMPLE OF NICODEMUS

Nicodemus was a wealthy man and a member of the Jerusalem Sanhedrin. The Sanhedrin was the ruling body of the Jews and was in charge of the government and discipline of their synagogues. Each town or synagogue had a Sanhedrin. The Sanhedrin in Jerusalem was the highest ruling body of the Jews, having authority over both spiritual and civil disputes of the Jewish people.[7] Nicodemus was a man of prestige and power. He came to Jesus by night so he would not be seen. Edersheim describes the scene:

It was night—one of the nights in that Easter week so full of marvels. . . . Up in the simply furnished Aliyah—the guest-chamber on the roof—the lamp was still burning, and the Heavenly Guest still busy with thought and words. There was no need for Nicodemus to pass through the house, for an outside stair led to the upper room. He had come because he recognized Jesus as "a teacher come from God; for no man can do these miracles that thou doest, except God be with him" (John 3:2).[8]

Nicodemus's curiosity was piqued. Jesus' miracles had stirred his soul, but he was not yet converted. Edersheim characterized many of Christ's followers in Jerusalem as sign-seekers who had a "milk faith" that required signs for its sustenance. These disciples were not like the Savior's first Galilean disciples, who had left everything to follow him. Instead, they had a more difficult time letting go of their worldly status and becoming converted to their Savior: "And yet He did, in wondrous love, condescend and speak to them in the only language they could understand, in that of 'signs.'"[9] Then, Edersheim makes a wonderful "we" comment: "We would not expect to be convinced of the truth of religion, nor converted to it, by outward miracles; we would not expect them at all."[10]

Nicodemus was dealing with the inner struggle of embracing Christ and, thus, leaving many of his Jewish beliefs. This was not an easy decision for Nicodemus to make, as it had not been easy for Edersheim, giving up everything, including associations, relationships, and a complete way of life. It truly meant a total rebirth:

> Judaism could understand a new relationship towards God and man, and even the forgiveness of sins. But it had no conception of a moral renovation, a spiritual birth, as the initial condition for reformation, far less as that for seeing the Kingdom of God. And it was because it had no idea of such "birth from above," of its reality or even possibility, that Judaism could not be the Kingdom of God. . . . Ours it is now only to "believe," where we cannot further know, and, looking up to the Son of Man in His perfected work, to perceive, and to receive the gift of God's love for our healing.[11]

Edersheim understood one must be converted and go through a similar renewal process to become a part of God's kingdom. A man can be learned as to secular knowledge, but Christ's instructions transcend worldly wisdom. Earthly acclaim is characterized by self-improvement, self-development, and self-restraint; but the Savior's teachings are centered on submission of our minds and hearts to him.

> And so it ever is with us also, when, like Nicodemus, we first arrive at the conviction that Jesus is the Teacher come from God. What He teaches is so entirely different from what Nicodemus, or any of us could, from any other standpoint other than that of Jesus, have learned or know concerning the Kingdom and entrance into it. . . . But to perceive this, not as an improvement upon our present state, but as the submission of heart, mind, and life to Him as our Divine King, an existence which is, and which means, proclaiming unto the world the Kingship of God: this can only be learned from Christ.[12]

In addition to understanding the nuances of Nicodemus's change, Edersheim looked to the symbolic nature of the setting of this story. Nicodemus was seeking light in the darkness and an understanding of spiritual rebirth during the springtime. These images of darkness and light, spring and rebirth, are inextricably connected with the eternal principles Christ was trying to teach. Edersheim explains in poetic simplicity how this night encounter is representative of the gospel message of Jesus Christ shining in the darkness: "Through the gusty night of our world's early spring flashes, as the lamp in that Aliyah through the darkened streets of silent Jerusalem, that light sounds through its stillness, like the Voice of the Teacher come from God."[13]

Christ's message during Nicodemus's night visit shone brightly in Edersheim's heart. He had a firm conviction that he would willingly give all for the Savior and within just a few years of his conversion, that conviction would again be tested.

## PREACHING THE GOSPEL OF JESUS CHRIST TO OTHERS

This was a period of great disruption in the Church of Scotland. In 1843, the church had divided into two camps: the Established Church and the Free Church. The disagreement was over the relationship between the civil government and the rights of the church. The Scottish civil courts would interfere with church decisions, even over appointments of ministers. The Free Church of Scotland was breaking free of any ties with the government. Dr. Duncan was a preacher in the Free Church of Scotland, and because of Edersheim's loyalty and love for his mentor and friend, he also became associated with the Free Church. He was very close to the Duncan family, even living with them for a time during his stay in Edinburgh.[14]

As a result of his combined theological studies in Germany and at New College and his previous university work in Vienna and Pest, Edersheim was given a theological degree and ordained to the ministry in 1846. As a minister for the Free Church of Scotland, Alfred was soon given responsibility over four small parishes in Edinburgh. This was hard work for young Edersheim. He would teach on Sundays wherever he could, without an established congregation or meeting house: "On Sundays, he would preach in three or four different places—barn, smithy, lay-loft, road."[15] After six months of hard work, he was able to consolidate his growing congregation and build a church building with a parsonage.

## "I HATE THE KIND OF
preaching which pretends to rearing mountains. In reality, they are only children making mud pies, which they call mountains."
—Alfred Edersheim

Always a great speaker, Edersheim had a way of making religion understandable and interesting for all his parishioners. Often he started with an empty church. After hearing his sermons, crowds would soon come and fill the pews until there was standing room only. He wrote, "I hate the kind of preaching which pretends to rearing mountains. In reality, they are only children making mud pies, which they call mountains."[16] His message of conversion was infectious and many loved to hear him speak. His daughter Ella described him thus: "Dr. Edersheim retained a vast fund of humour . . . and an intense interest in all the questions of life—political, scientific, domestic. His conversation was of a peculiarly brilliant order, sparkling with epigram and illustration."[17]

Less than a year after he had started preaching for the Free Church, Alfred developed a great longing to work among the Jews. In the latter part of 1846, he felt a call from God to serve as a missionary to his people. Based on this prompting, he resigned from his ministerial post in Edinburgh and traveled the long road through Greece and Constantinople to the province of Moldavia in Romania, a hub of Jewish culture and activities. He preached Christianity for over a year[18] to the large population of Russian Jews who had migrated there to escape persecution from the czar. It was during this time that he met his future wife, Mary Broomfield, from Scotland, who was also a missionary to the Jews. After returning to Scotland in 1847, Alfred and Mary wed on February 28, 1848.

In a matter of four years Alfred Edersheim had gone from a young Jewish scholar and translator to an ordained Christian minister, intent on further studying the gospel of Jesus Christ. In the process he had left behind close family associations and rich tradition all for his Savior. After having a church built for him, a privilege some ministers wait for their whole lives, Edersheim again left everything when he felt prompted by the Spirit. It is clear through his action that Edersheim understood what the psalmist wrote:

> The law of the Lord is perfect, converting the soul:
> the testimony of the Lord is sure, making wise the simple.
> The statues of the Lord are right, rejoicing the heart:
> the commandment of the Lord is pure, enlightening the eyes.
> (Psalm 19:7–8)

# NOTES

1. Edersheim, *Jesus the Messiah*, 269 (1:388). For the references in Edersheim's *Jesus the Messiah*, I have included the book and approximate page number in the original edition of the book (book 1 or book 2, with the page number after the colon) in parentheses after the page number in the reprint used in the more recent edition cited in the bibliography. In the recent edition, both books are printed as one volume.
2. Edersheim, *Tohu-va-Vohu*, xiv.
3. Mayhew, "Alfred Edersheim," 176–77.
4. Mayhew, "Alfred Edersheim," 178.
5. Neander, *General History of the Christian Religion and Church*, vi.

6. Edersheim, *Lectures*, ix.
7. Edersheim, *Jesus the Messiah*, 265 (1:384).
8. Edersheim, *Sketches*, 256–57.
9. Edersheim, *Jesus the Messiah*, 262 (1:379).
10. Edersheim, *Jesus the Messiah*, 262 (1:379).
11. Edersheim, *Jesus the Messiah*, 266–68 (1:385–87).
12. Edersheim, *Jesus the Messiah*, 266 (1:385).
13. Edersheim, *Jesus the Messiah*, 269 (1:388).
14. Mayhew, "Alfred Edersheim," 175.
15. Edersheim, *Tohu-va-Vohu*, xv.
16. Edersheim, *Tohu-va-Vohu*, 86.
17. Edersheim, *Tohu-va-Vohu*, xxxii.
18. Mayhew, "Alfred Edersheim," 179.

# CHAPTER THREE

# "LORD, TO WHOM SHALL WE GO?"

AFTER FEEDING THE FIVE thousand with five barley loaves and two small fishes, the Savior asked his Apostles to gather the excess. They found that they had twelve baskets of food left over. The multitude was amazed and kept following the Savior, hoping for more physical food rather than the spiritual food given through his teachings. They wanted a tangible miracle instead of the miracle of a changed heart.

The Savior censored them: "Verily, verily, I say unto you, Ye seek me, not because ye saw the miracles, but because ye did eat of the loaves and were filled" (John 6:26).

What followed is commonly referred to as the Bread of Life sermon. Christ lovingly and forcefully tried to teach his disciples what they should be seeking. They had expected a Messiah who would be a warrior-king saving them from political oppression and giving them back the fat of the land. Instead, the Savior taught that his disciples must surrender themselves to his will and become his meek and humble followers. Like the miraculous bread the multitude had eaten, the manna their fathers ate in the wilderness did not bring them eternal life. Eventually they died despite participating in such a great miracle. But his holy sacrament would bring eternal life to their bodies and to the souls.

The Savior taught, "Verily, verily, I say unto you, He that believeth on

17

me hath everlasting life. I am that bread of life. Your fathers did eat manna in the wilderness and are dead. . . . Except ye eat the flesh of the Son of man, and drink his blood, ye have no life in you" (John 6:47–49, 53).

These words sounded most mysterious to many in the multitude.[1] Those who heard it had a difficult time understanding, and some who did understand his words did not want to believe them. Therefore, many of Jesus' disciples said, "This is an hard saying; who can hear it?" (John 6:60). Offended by Jesus' teachings, they turned away from following the Savior. Edersheim characterized this moment as "the great crisis in the History of Christ."[2] This was an hour of decision and a parting for many. Christ had clearly set forth the highest truths concerning himself in direct opposition to the multitude's views about their Messiah.

Now the Jewish people had to decide whether Jesus was really their Messiah. His works seemed to prove it; yet his words seemed incongruous to the Messiah-king they had been hoping for. For many, their decision that day was that Jesus was not their long-awaited king or one they would accept. But more significantly, for the first time this struggle was not confined to the multitude. It had reached into the hearts of the Twelve. Would they also turn and leave him?

 "LORD, TO WHOM SHALL WE GO?
Thou has the words of eternal life" (John 6:67).
This simple testimony was initially spoken by Peter.
Edersheim also felt the power of these words.

Edersheim explained that this was the first Gethsemane-like incident for the true followers of Jesus and his Twelve Apostles.[3] It was a point in time where their conversion to Jesus Christ, as their Messiah, was sorely tested. Jesus turned to his Twelve Apostles and asked the poignant and searching question: "Will ye also go away?" (John 6:67).

Simon Peter, the chief Apostle, answered for the Twelve: "Lord, to whom shall we go? Thou hast the words of eternal life. And we believe and are sure that thou art that Christ, the Son of the living God" (John 6:68–69).

Peter's sentiments expressed Edersheim's "inmost conviction of mind and heart."[4] Although Edersheim would experience doubt and confusion in terms of his feelings toward dogma, his conviction that Christianity was true would never falter. Health and other trials would also force him to make life decisions that would affect his family and professional life, but he had made the greater decision to become a disciple of Christ, no matter how difficult the way. His testimony of Christ's teaching would be tried to its very foundations, yet he would remain true.

In answer to the Savior's inquiry, Peter's question-response, "Lord, to whom shall we go?" and subsequent unwavering testimony was a theme in Edersheim's writings. Obviously, Edersheim had felt the Lord asking him the same question regarding his allegiance, but his answer was as sure as Peter's. He remembered his initial spiritual experience and held on to what he knew was true. Thus, his faith continued to grow stronger and stronger, even during times of trial:

> It is thus, also, that many of us, whose thoughts may have been sorely tossed, and whose foundations terribly assailed, may have found our first resting-place in the assured, unassailable spiritual experience of the past. Whither can we go for Words of Eternal Life, if not to Christ? If He fails us, then all hope of the Eternal is gone. But He has the Words of Eternal life—and we believed when they first came to us; nay, we know that He is the Holy One of God. And this conveys all that faith needs for further learning.[5]

## OLD ABERDEEN

After Alfred and Mary's wedding, they went back to Aberdeen, Scotland, in 1848. He became an assistant minister in the Aberdeen area and within four months was asked to serve as minister of the Old Aberdeen parish, where he would minister until 1860. He also began teaching at the local university.

EDERSHEIM WAS A minister for over ten years at The Free Church of Scotland at Aberdeen.

A period of intense theological study and writing followed Edersheim's appointment at Old Aberdeen. His early publications were translations of Latin and German works[6] and theological articles for journals such as the *Athenaeum* and the *British and Foreign Review*.[7] Soon, though, he authored four major works of his own that were biblical and church histories.[8] Alfred and Mary also had seven children during these years: Stephanie, Mary, Julia, Marcia, Alfred Jr., Elise, and Madeleine.[9] Things were looking up for the growing family as Edersheim proved himself to be a popular preacher and talented writer. He was hopeful that he would get an appointment as a professor of theology at the University of Aberdeen.

Due to these intense gospel and philosophical studies, Edersheim began to question the Christian sect to which he belonged. His sympathies were leaning toward a more universal Church. The squabbles between the various factions of the Church of Scotland did not ring true as he thought about the teachings of the Savior. The kingdom of God was for all mankind and there should not be splintering factions. As he expressed his views to others, he met with extreme opposition in Scotland, experiencing "more than one threat of persecution."[10] Ironically, it was not his Jewish heritage that caused him to be persecuted by others. Instead, it was his questioning of sectarian views in the Free Church of Scotland.

## TORQUAY

During the winter of 1860–61, Alfred Edersheim's health became very poor with a chest cold. His doctors and friends encouraged him to quit Old Aberdeen and seek a milder climate. Heeding their advice, Alfred moved his family to Torquay in the southwest of England. Once more, he became "a stranger in a strange land, with broken health, with little or no means."[11] This time he was not alone, but had a large family to support.

After mending for a few weeks in Torquay, the manager of the hotel where the family was staying invited Edersheim to give a Sunday sermon at the hotel. Within three weeks, the room was overflowing. The Scottish residents of the town asked Edersheim to pastor for them. The land was immediately donated and funds were raised for a new church and parish. St. Andrew, the name of the church, was built, and Edersheim moved his family there. After a few years, there was a thriving congregation. Edersheim and his family would enjoy ten happy years in Torquay.

Edersheim wrote little during this time because he was so busy establishing a new congregation. A few short books and pamphlets were published, including one about the life of Elisha the prophet, and several children's books. Another child also joined the family, Ella.[12] Ella was very close to her father. She would later compile her father's journal notes and add her own sketch of his life in a book called *Tohu-va-Vohu* (taken from the Hebrew, meaning "without form and void," as in Genesis 1:2). This was published posthumously in 1890 and is the only source document on Edersheim's life.

While at St. Andrews, Edersheim worked hard at ministering to the community, "giving of his best for the service of God."[13] He loved teaching and preaching, not only sharing his testimony with his parishioners, but also with his own older brother, Julius Edersheim. In 1868, he had the opportunity to teach his brother about Jesus Christ. Julius accepted the message and was christened by Reverend Edersheim in his church at Torquay on September 23, 1868. The time in Torquay seemed to be full of family, work, and accomplishment, but tragedy would strike here too. Sadly, the family suffered the great loss of their wife and mother, Mary. This must have been a very difficult time for Edersheim with so many young children still to raise. Their seven daughters and one son needed a mother, so Edersheim remarried quickly. Later that year, Alfred married Sophia Hancock, the youngest daughter of a local admiral.

EDERSHEIM WOULD GIVE "his best for the service of God" at the St. Andrew Cathedral.

By 1870, Edersheim's health was again poor. He wintered in San Remo, Italy, and Menton, France. During his stay there, his health never completely recovered. Unable to fulfill his responsibilities at Torquay, he resigned in 1872 and moved his family to Bournemouth in the south of England, building a villa there. He optimistically dubbed the home *Heniach*, meaning "The Lord will give rest," hoping for better health and a better life for his family.[14]

# NOTES

1. Edersheim, *Jesus the Messiah*, 498 (2:35). Edersheim goes through six points of why this sermon would have been so mysterious to the Jewish followers. See book 3 chapter 32 entitled, "The Great Crisis in Popular Feeling—The Last Discourses in the Synagogue of Capernaum—Christ the Bread of Life—'Will Ye Also Go Away?'"

2. Edersheim, *Jesus the Messiah*, 499 (2:36).

3. Edersheim, *Jesus the Messiah*, 499 (2:36).

4. Edersheim, *Jesus the Messiah*, xvi.

5. Edersheim, *Jesus the Messiah*, 499 (2:36). This story meant so much to Edersheim that he referenced it in his introductory remarks in *Jesus the Messiah*. "The confession of this inmost conviction of mind and heart: 'Lord, to Whom shall we go? The words of eternal life hast Thou! And we have believed and know that Thou art the Holy One of God'" (xvi).

6. The German translations included J. Henry Kurtz's well-known *History of the Old Covenant* and *History of the Christian Church to the Reformation*. Edersheim also translated Peter Lange's *Commentary on Matthew*.

7. Mayhew, "Alfred Edersheim," 181.

8. These are: *History of the Jewish Nation After the Destruction of Jerusalem by Titus* (1856); *The History of Israel and Judah from the Decline of the Two Kingdoms to the Assyrian and Babylonian Captivity* (1857); *Bohemian Reformers and German Politicians: A Contribution to the History of Protestantism* (1858); and *History of the Jewish Nation from the Fall of Jerusalem to the Reign of Constantine the Great* (1861); see Mayhew, "Alfred Edersheim," 182.

9. Mayhew, "Alfred Edersheim," 182.

10. Edersheim, *Tohu-va-Vohu*, xix.

11. Edersheim, *Tohu-va-Vohu*, xx.

12. Mayhew, "Alfred Edersheim," 183.

13. Edersheim, *Tohu-va-Vohu*, xx.

14. Mayhew, "Alfred Edersheim," 183.

# Chapter Four

# "Trials Are God's Veiled Angels"

The Talmud tells of an old Jewish man who stopped by the road to pray. In the middle of his prayer, a soldier passed by and greeted the man. The old man did not stop his prayer to acknowledge the soldier. The soldier was furious. He waited until the old man was finished praying and then reprimanded him for being so thoughtless. He warned him that he, as a soldier, had every right to behead him for not returning his greeting. The man asked for the soldier's forgiveness. Then he tried to explain his seemingly rude behavior.

"If you were in the presence of your king, and a friend came by for a casual chat, would you respond to your friend?"

"No, not in the presence of the king," replied the soldier. "If I did, the king would execute me for sure."

The man answered the soldier, "If that's how you would act in the presence of a worldly king, a mere man, consider my options when you approached me. How much more was I compelled to behave as I did when praying before my King of Kings and my God?"[1]

Even though the world, as symbolized by the soldier, may not realize or acknowledge who the King of Kings is, Edersheim knew him and put his entire life on the line for his testimony of the Savior. Often he had to give up his will to accomplish the things the Lord had in store for him.

Edersheim experienced many years of poor health from living and serving in Scotland's wet, bleak climate. These years of physical struggle were a trial for him, yet he soon discovered that "trials are God's veiled angels to us."[2] Although his bouts of sickness forced him to resign from ministering to the people he loved, it did free up his time to write, leaving a legacy that would lift future scholars and Saints. The harsh cold winters of the British Isles were difficult, and he would get sick easily, for his lungs were not strong. During times of bad health, he would go some place warm and write, but eventually he would return to his duties as a minister.

Finally, his health would not permit even that. When he left Torquay, he not only struggled physically with his health but emotionally with leaving his flock, financially with losing his source of income, and spiritually with making a significant change from being affiliated with the Church of Scotland to the Church of England. These times of trial gave him further empathy for the trials and suffering of others, even a glimpse into the pain and suffering of the Savior himself. He remembered the Savior's promise: "In me ye might have peace. In the world ye shall have tribulations: but be of good cheer, I have overcome the world" (John 16:33). Edersheim expressed this "good cheer" in the midst of struggle when he said, "We speak of joys departed, never to return, And yet no real joy ever wholly departs, but leaves on the heart a sweet memory of peace. And is not the afterglow more beautiful even than the bright sunlight? Oh, to carry with us an afterglow of life into another world!"[3] Rather than allowing himself to be depressed, he looked up to see the miracle, blessing, and peace of this period of his life. Yet even with this eternal perspective, coping with the realities of his health and making such sweeping life changes was challenging. In his personal journal, he reflected, "I have found it most difficult of all simply to submit to God, and not to try to direct my own destinies."[4]

### The Temple: Its Ministry and Services at the Time of Jesus Christ (1874)

As reverend of St. Andrews, Edersheim had not had much time to study and write. Now, he dived into an intensive study of the Talmud and other Jewish writings, resulting in a book still very popular today:

*The Temple: Its Ministry and Services at the Time of Jesus Christ* (1874). His purpose in writing this book was "to take the reader back nineteen centuries; to show him Jerusalem as it was, when our Lord passed through its streets, and the Sanctuary, when He taught in its porches and courts; to portray, not only the appearance and structure of the Temple, but to describe its ordinances and worshippers, the ministries of its priesthood, and the ritual of its services."[5]

Jesus' life revolved around the temple in Jerusalem, from Anna and Simeon's testimony of his divinity eight days after his birth to the veil rent at the moment of his death. Jewish temple worship was punctuated by the yearly feasts and festivals. In his book on the temple, Edersheim described each feast and festival, explained the Jewish traditions associated with them, and placed them in the context of the life and ministry of Jesus Christ. Edersheim preserved and communicated the cultural and religious customs of the Israelites, revealing the powerful spiritual context of these events.

After having read Edersheim's book on the temple, Sir George Williams of Cambridge University, who was also the founder of the Young Men's Christian Association (YMCA),[6] sought him out, and they became close friends. Edersheim confided to Williams about his changing convictions concerning the Free Church of Scotland and his desire to obtain priestly orders in the Church of England.

Using his influence, Sir Williams made it possible for Dr. Edersheim to become a licensed preacher in the Church of England in 1876. Edersheim wrote, "I have passed from the Scotch to the English Church and have not for one moment regretted the change. The changing was and is most unpleasant, but not the change; that has placed me where all my sympathies find most ample scope."[7]

During his service with the Church of England, he served as vicar at Loders, a Warburtonian lecturer at Lincoln's Inn in London, and a select preacher at the University of Oxford.

### Sketches of Jewish Social Life in the Days of Christ (1876)

In 1876, the same year he became a minister in the Church of England, Edersheim published another popular book, *Sketches of Jewish Social Life in the Days of Christ.* Similar to his book on the temple in Jerusalem, this book was to "transport the reader into the land of

Palestine at the time of our Lord and of His apostles."[8] Edersheim described Palestine two millennia ago, the Jews and Gentiles in the land, Galilee during Christ's time, Jewish homes, families, society, and the various Jewish sects and their worship.

**THE MEZUZAH IS A SMALL,** metal case attached to the doorpost of a home, enclosing parchment on which scripture passages are written.

Edersheim gives many examples of Jewish life during the time of Christ. While describing the closeness of a Jewish family, Edersheim highlights the great responsibility parents in Israel felt to teach their young children the Jewish religion. Between the ages of five and six, Jewish children were expected to start reading and studying the Old Testament. But even before learning to speak or read, they would be a part of the family prayers, the rites of the Sabbath, and the festival seasons. Jewish children would watch their parents reverently touch the *mezuzah*, and then kiss their finger that had touched it, every time they entered their home, learning from infancy respect for the scriptures.

The mezuzah, also the Hebrew word for "doorpost," was a small, metal case enclosing a longitudinally folded parchment square on which two passages were written (Deuteronomy 6:4–9; 11:13–21). The case was attached to the entering doorpost of their home: "The child, when carried in arms, would naturally put out its hand to it; the more so, that it would see the father and all others, on going out or in, reverently touch the case, and afterwards kiss the finger, speaking at the same time a benediction."[9] This simple act would teach Jewish children to reverence the Torah, or the Law, and to "love the Lord your God, and to serve him with all your heart and with all your soul."[10] Edersheim himself had been raised in a loving Jewish home where the law was reverenced. He had learned to read and study the scriptures. These early lessons from childhood influenced the course of his entire life.

### Bible History: Old Testament (1876–1887)

Between the years of 1876 and 1887, Edersheim published seven volumes of *Bible History: Old Testament*. Starting from the Creation and ending with the final prophecies of Jeremiah, Edersheim wrote this work for "those who teach and those who learn, whether in the school or in the family."[11] He encouraged young and old, advanced scholar and Sunday School teacher, to use this book as a resource in teaching the Bible. He studied the sacred text in the original Hebrew; he cited Bible studies in German and English; and he studied biblical geography, antiquities, and Egyptian and Assyrian monuments for this work. After this intense research, Edersheim came to the conclusion: "But when all has been done, the feeling grows only more strong that there is another and higher understanding of the Bible, without which all else is vain. Not merely to know the meaning of the narratives of Scripture, but to realize their spiritual application . . . this is the only profitable study of Scripture."[12]

Edersheim emphasized the need for the Messiah throughout all the biblical text, starting from the Fall of Adam. Men could choose to accept this hope through symbolic religious rites and covenants that reminded them of their faith in a Savior or Deliverer: "The promise which God freely gave to man was that of a Deliverer, who would bruise the head of the serpent, and destroy his works."[13]

Yet there were men who would not embrace this promise. Instead, these people would "naturally choose the world as it then was,"[14] savoring its pleasures and lusts. Edersheim explained the sons of Adam, Cain and Abel, are examples of two people choosing these divergent paths. Abel's sacrifice was one of obedience that reminded him of a path of faith to the Lord. Cain and his people would try to distort these truths by sacrificing in a different way than that which had been taught or commanded by the Lord.

Listening to the Lord's prophets and obeying their words helps those who want to follow this path of truth. They are taught "the light of His Gospel, which teaches them 'the way, the truth, and the life,' even Him who is 'the Lamb of God, which taketh away the sin of the world.' "[15] This theme of obedience and disobedience and looking forward to the Deliverer is carried throughout Edersheim's commentary of the Old Testament.

# THE WARBURTON LECTURES

are a series of religious guest lectures at Lincoln's
Inn Chapel at Cambridge University. The first
series of lectures was given by Richard Hurd
(1720–1808). They are still continued today.

### *Prophecy and History in Relation to the Messiah* (1885)

During this time of intense study, Edersheim gave a series of lectures between the years of 1880 and 1884 which were then published in 1885 as a book entitled *Prophecy and History in Relation to the Messiah: The Warburton Lectures for 1880–1884.* The main object of these lectures was to prove the truth of Christianity through the use of the Old Testament and the origin of Christianity as being established in the Old Testament. He discussed at great length New Testament writers looking back to the Old Testament for prophecies of Jesus Christ as the Messiah. He analyzed the messianic hope of the Israelites and the idea of the kingdom of God. Finally, he reviewed the teachings of John the Baptist as a segue between the Old and New Testaments.[16] There were also two appendices on the arrangement and analysis of the Pentateuch, or the first five books of the Old Testament.

His lectures read differently than his formally written books. The reader gains a better feel for Edersheim as a great lecturer, not just a writer. His testimony of the Savior is still at the center of his words. Edersheim focused on three questions in his lectures:

1. Is there any real prophecy in the Old Testament?
2. Were these prophets really prophets in Israel sent by God?
3. Was there any messianic hope in the Old Testament?

Edersheim showed how the prophets of the Old Testament prophesied of future events, focusing on the coming of the Messiah and the kingdom of God. By establishing the truthfulness of the Old Testament prophecies, the fulfillment of the coming of Christ is confirmed; but "with the rejection of prophecy in the Old Testament the claims of Christ, as set forth in the New Testament, fall to the ground."[17] Edersheim concludes that the "whole Old Testament is prophetic . . . and all prophecy points to the Kingdom of God and to the Messiah as its King."[18] This is all in keeping with the major points of Edersheim's testimony of the Bible, that "the New Testament is the organic development and completion of the Old."[19]

### The Life and Times of Jesus the Messiah (1883)

Edersheim's most famous work, *The Life and Times of Jesus the Messiah*, was published in 1883. In its preface, Edersheim noted, "All my previous studies were really in preparation for this."[20]

He tried to present the facts of Jesus' life, disclaiming any predetermined dogmatic viewpoint, delivering, "as far as we can, the truth, irrespective of consequences."[21] Yet this did not stop him from declaring his personal testimony about Jesus Christ: "Admittedly, He was the One perfect Man—the ideal of humanity; His doctrine the one absolute teaching. The world has known none other, none equal."[22]

In 1876, he moved to the rural village of Loders to begin his work on his magnum opus. It took him seven years of continual and earnest labor to write this book. He was in a remote country parish, isolated from "all social intercourse, and amidst not a few trials"[23] while studying and writing this work. When he got to a point that was difficult or needed further investigation, he could give it days of undisturbed work. His daughter Ella helped him index the work and read the copy proofs for errors.

Edersheim had a particular interest in portraying Jesus as a Jew living in Palestine, Jesus' intellectual and religious development, and his Hebraic "surroundings of place, society, and popular life."[24] Edersheim's love of the Jewish culture and traditions and lands are expressed in his descriptions of the Savior. His love for Jerusalem continued to his death. Even though he died many miles away, he was buried "looking straight towards Jerusalem, the city whose people he loved and tried to serve."[25]

"OURS IT IS NOW ONLY to believe, where we cannot further know, and looking up to the Son of Man in His perfected work, to perceive, and to receive the gift of God's love for our healing."
—Alfred Edersheim

For Edersheim, the Savior's life started miraculously and ended miraculously. His wonder and awe are felt throughout his descriptions of the Savior's life: "They who would write a Life of Christ aright must themselves also begin (in heart and soul) as the Gospels begin—with the angels' song, the worship of the shepherds, and the gifts of the Magi. Or, if they would preach to us from it they must begin like John with this: 'Behold the Lamb of God, which taketh away the sin of the world.' "[26]

## EDERSHEIM FACES ANTI-SEMITICISM

In his second preface to *The Life and Time of Jesus the Messiah*, Edersheim expressed his pleasure with how well the book was received, except for "one element of pain."[27] Ironically, his book had been said to be anti-Semitic. Even today, current readers have made similar comments about his descriptions of the Jews and their treatment of Jesus Christ. Personally, Edersheim disagreed with these negative characterizations of his work: "That any such thought could possibly attach to a book concerning Him, Who was Himself a Jew; Who in the love of his compassion wept tears of bitter anguish over the Jerusalem that was about to crucify Him, and Whose first utterance and prayer when nailed to the Cross was: 'Father, forgive them, for they know not what they do'—would seem terribly incongruous and painful."[28]

He felt that the love of Christ promoted feelings that were the antithesis of the Anti-Semitic Movement spreading across pre-WWI Europe, breeding feelings of "envy, jealousy, and cupidity on the one hand; or on the other, ignorance, prejudice bigotry, and hatred of race,"[29] and he hoped that his books would soften attitudes toward covenant Jews.

An example of a passage from Edersheim's book that is mistakenly characterized for its anti-Semitic sentiments was Edersheim's commentary on the statement of the Jews when Pilate asked, "Shall I crucify your King? The chief priests answered, We have no king but Caesar" (John 19:15). Edersheim wrote, "With this cry Judaism was, in the person of its representatives, guilty of denial of God, of blasphemy, of apostasy. It committed suicide; and ever since, has its dead body been carried in show from land to land, and from century to century: to be dead and to remain dead till He come a second time Who is the Resurrection and the Life!"[30] Some have felt this is a rather harsh statement made by Edersheim, passing unjust judgment on the atrocities that have been done to the Jewish people for the last two millennia, when nothing could be further from the truth.

As a young man, Edersheim had experienced anti-Semitism from others in his community. He understood what it meant to feel this unjust hatred and persecution. After his conversion to Christianity, he still believed strongly in the calling of Israel as the covenant people. He recognized in the outward rituals of his youth the signs of the Savior. He especially encouraged Christians to gain a love of the Old Testament. Edersheim wrote, "I feel convinced that the real root of anti-Semitism is depreciation of the Old Testament. If we have low opinions of the Old Testament we shall come to despise and to hate the Jews and perhaps not unreasonably so. Love for the Old Testament leads to love for Israel."[31]

Edersheim loved his Jewish heritage. Until the end of his life, he sought to return to his beloved homeland and always felt a sense of mission to serve his people.

### Tohu-va-Vohu (Without Form and Void) (1890)

*Tohu-va-Vohu* is the title for Edersheim's random thoughts taken from his diary, started in 1870. This work was published posthumously in 1890 with a short memoir written by his daughter Ella. The title is Hebrew, meaning "without form and void," and is taken from Genesis 1:2: "And the earth was without form and void; and darkness was upon the face of the deep. And the Spirit of God moved upon the face of the waters." There is no organization to his thoughts in this book. Yet there are many important insights and enlightening epiphanies. Here are a few examples:

All I really know of God—all I want to know of God—is in Christ. My God is only God in Christ; I know no other, and I do not want to know any other than as there revealed.[32]

With reverence be it said: Our modern theology has almost lost sight of the Father. Our thoughts and our prayers are almost exclusively directed to the Second Person of the Godhead. Yet it is to the Father we are to come through the Son and by the Holy Spirit; and it was the object of the Son to reveal the Father, through the Holy Spirit given unto us.[33]

Somehow the tempter must have knowledge of our thoughts, since his temptations are so adapted to them. I do not believe he can search our minds and hearts; but I suppose he can read our actual thinking, which is printed mind, as it were, just as we read the pages of a book.[34]

## DEATH AND THE AFTERLIFE

While growing up, Edersheim had been taught conflicting views about death and the afterlife. Edersheim wrote, "Never are the voices of the Rabbis more discordant, and their utterances more contradictory or unsatisfying than in view of the great problems of humanity: sin, sickness, death and the hereafter."[35] The Jews have had contradictory views about the resurrection for many millennia. During the time of Christ, the Sadducees held that there could be "no bodily resurrection."[36] This was in direct opposition to the belief of the Pharisees and other Jews of this period.

Edersheim quoted the Rabbi Eliezer saying, "Repent on the day before thou diest. His disciples asked him: Can a man know the hour of his death? He replied: Therefore let him repent today, lest haply he die on the morrow."[37] Edersheim realized the necessity of preparing for death by developing what was inside of him. He wrote, "It is a fallacy to suppose that age brings wisdom or knowledge. The lapse of time adds nothing to our potentiality; it only develops what is in us. At the age of sixty a man is either a perfect fool, or he ought to have a good deal of sense."[38]

On March 18, 1889, at the age of sixty-four, Alfred Edersheim was in the town of Mentone on the Italian Riviera trying to recover from another bout of bad health. It was a place that he loved. Its olive groves and blue sky reminded him of the Holy Land. For five short months,

*Death*

he seemed to be improving in health and was planning a journey home, when "God's finger touched him and he slept."[39]

His final entry in *Tohu-va-Vohu* is unfinished. His last written words were: "We are reproached that we treat not the historical documents of the Bible in exactly the same manner as the ordinary history of those times in which the miraculous and the legendary are accepted. Now there are here two points of view . . ."[40] The sentence is left hanging. As his obituary in the *London Times* described, his death was sudden: "His health had been seriously affected for some time, but it was not anticipated that his illness would have so sudden a termination."[41]

Through a life of faith, service, study, and reflection, Edersheim had been healed; even though his body had not been physically well, his spirit was strong. He had a great hope for a life after this earthly existence. Edersheim wrote, "The tears of earth's night hang as dewdrops on flower and tree, presently to sparkle like diamonds in the morning sun. For in that night of nights has Christ mingled the sweat of human toil and sorrow with the precious blood of His agony, and made it drop on earth as sweet balsam to heal its wounds, to soothe its sorrows, and to take away its death."[42]

He lived life well, following his own axiom "Live slowly your life: its joys and its sorrows; its toil and its rest. He must eat slowly that would digest well."[43] He looked forward to the Messiah and was reborn in his testimony that Jesus is the Christ. Now, he is with Him and "beholds his King in all His beauty."[44]

His search for a universal church has now been realized. The fact that he did not hear the restored gospel of Jesus Christ in this life has surely been rectified, perhaps by the very Apostles and LDS scholars who benefited from his prolific pen. Elder Bruce R. McConkie expressed:

> The hope—nay, offer the prayer—that . . . Edersheim, and others who had faith and believed in the Messiah, according to the best light and knowledge they had, now that they are in the world of spirits where Elder Talmage continues his apostolic ministry, may have received added light and knowledge and will have pursued that strait and narrow course that will make them inheritors of the fulness of our Father's kingdom. Truly they were Eliases of a greater day and harbingers of a greater light.[45]

# NOTES

1. Bleefeld and Shook, *Save the World Entire*, 207 (Talmudic source: *Berachot* 32).
2. Edersheim, *Tohu-va-Vohu*, 49
3. Edersheim, *Tohu-va-Vohu*, 49.
4. Edersheim, *Tohu-va-Vohu*, 34.
5. Edersheim, *The Temple*, vii.
6. Springhall, "Sir George Williams," 192.
7. Edersheim, *Tohu-va-Vohu*, 44–45.
8. Edersheim, *Sketches*, vii.
9. Edersheim, *Sketches*, 102.
10. Deuteronomy 11:13—"And it shall come to pass, if ye shall hearken diligently unto my commandments which I command you this day, to love the Lord your God, and to serve him with all your heart and with all your soul."
11. Edersheim, *Bible History*, 3.
12. Edersheim, *Bible History*, 4.
13. Edersheim, *Bible History*, 17.
14. Edersheim, *Bible History*, 17.
15. Edersheim, *Bible History*, 18.
16. To be discussed in more detail at the end of chapter 8 in this book.
17. Edersheim, *Lectures*, 55.
18. Edersheim, *Lectures*, 24.
19. Edersheim, *Lectures*, 26.
20. Edersheim, *Jesus the Messiah*, xv.
21. Edersheim, *Jesus the Messiah*, xii.
22. Edersheim, *Jesus the Messiah*, 127 (1:180).
23. Edersheim, *Jesus the Messiah*, xv.
24. Edersheim, *Jesus the Messiah*, xi.
25. Edersheim, *Tohu-va-Vohu*, xxvii.
26. Edersheim, *Tohu-va-Vohu*, 30.
27. Edersheim, *Jesus the Messiah*, xvii.
28. Edersheim, *Jesus the Messiah*, xvii.
29. Edersheim, *Jesus the Messiah*, xvii.
30. Edersheim, *Jesus the Messiah*, 874 (2:581).
31. Edersheim, *Tohu-va-Vohu*, 78.
32. Edersheim, *Tohu-va-Vohu*, 11.
33. Edersheim, *Tohu-va-Vohu*, 14.
34. Edersheim, *Tohu-va-Vohu*, 17.
35. Edersheim, *Sketches*, 149.

36. Talmage, *Jesus the Christ*, 547.

37. Edersheim, *Sketches*, 165.

38. Edersheim, *Tohu-va-Vohu*, 99.

39. Edersheim, *Tohu-va-Vohu*, xxviii.

40. Edersheim, *Tohu-va-Vohu*, 130.

41. *London Times*, Obituary, "Alfred Edersheim," 1889, 20.

42. Edersheim, *Sketches*, 166.

43. Edersheim, *Tohu-va-Vohu*, 59.

44. Edersheim, *Tohu-va-Vohu*, xxviii. These are the last words of Ella Edersheim in her memoir describing her father's death.

45. McConkie, *The Mortal Messiah*, 4:180, footnote 1.

# PART TWO

# THE WORKS OF ALFRED EDERSHEIM

*"So high an authority as Edersheim."*
—ELDER BRIGHAM HENRY ROBERTS

This part of the book is a concise discussion of the most fundamental concepts presented throughout Edersheim's writings. He wrote from the Jewish point of view while explaining the traditions and beliefs of the Old Testament and the temple ceremonies. Yet his recognition of their fulfillment is centered on the divinity of Jesus Christ.

# CHAPTER FIVE

# SCRIPTURES ARE THE LIFE OF THE SOUL

DURING CHRIST'S LIFETIME, MANY Jews spoke Greek because of the Hellenization of the known world. Latin was also often learned by necessity because Israel was a member of the Roman Empire. But rabbis did not study other worldly subjects, such as heathen science and literature. This was not allowed. To illustrate this point, Edersheim told a story about a young rabbi who thought he had time enough to study other things in addition to the scriptures. He asked an older rabbi if he could study Greek wisdom since he had read and studied the law and felt he knew it all. The older man reminded him about what Joshua wrote: "This book of the law shall not depart out of thy mouth; but thou shalt meditate therein day and night" (Joshua 1:8). While reflecting on this scripture, he said to the young man, "Go then, and consider which is the hour that is neither of the day nor of the night and in it thou mayest study Grecian wisdom."[1]

After telling this story, Edersheim continued, "It is to this day repeated each morning in his prayers by every Jew: 'These are the things of which a man eats the fruit of this world, but their possession continueth for the next world: to honour father and mother, pious works, peacemaking between man and man, and the study of the law, which is equivalent to them all.' "[2]

For the practicing Jew of Jesus' time, studying the scriptures was equal to all the knowledge of the world. Each morning, he prayed for God to help him do good works and study his law, which was equivalent to all the other good works he could do.[3] Even honoring parents, being a peacemaker, and performing religious devotions were seen as merely appendages to scriptural wisdom. Edersheim explains, "To the pious Jew . . . the knowledge of God was everything; and to prepare for or impart that knowledge was the sum total, the sole object of his education. This was the life of his soul—the better, the only true life, to which all else as well as the life of the body were merely subservient means towards an end."[4]

Edersheim's love of the scriptures came from his Jewish background. He would have been taught from the time he was a young child that the scriptures were a treasure to cherish. In his childhood home, the scriptures would have been prized as a great blessing from God. In his Jewish school connected to the local synagogue, Edersheim would have been taught from the Torah and learned the Jewish law. Even though Edersheim studied the secular wisdom and philosophy of his day, his heart and mind hastily returned to studying the scriptures. Later in his life, he would go back to the Jewish writings of the Talmud to help him better understand the Jewish background of the Old and New Testaments. During times of bad health, Edersheim found great inner strength from scripture reading.

## THE TORAH AND THE SEPTUAGINT

The focus of Jewish scripture study was the Torah, which means in Hebrew "law" or "instruction." The Torah consists of the first five books of Moses, also commonly called the Pentateuch, a Greek term meaning "the five-parted book" or "the five scroll containers in which the books were kept." The English names of these five books bear the title given by Greek translators of Hebrew scripture in the second to third century BC. These titles are descriptive of each book's contents. In the Hebrew Old Testament, the Jewish designation for each book is by the first or else the most prominent word that begins each book.[5]

- Genesis (*Bereshit*: "In the beginning . . .")
- Exodus (*Shemot*: "Names")
- Leviticus (*Vayyiqra*: "And he called . . .")
- Numbers (*Bamidbar*: "In the desert . . .")
- Deuteronomy (*Devarim*: "Words," or "Discourses")

The other two parts of Hebrew scripture are the Prophets:
- **The major prophets**—Joshua, Judges, 1 and 2 Samuel, 1 and 2 Kings, Isaiah, Jeremiah, Ezekiel.
- **The twelve minor prophets** (labeled minor because of their page length not their scriptural significance)—Hosea, Joel, Amos, Obadiah, Jonah, Micah, Nahum, Habakkuk, Zephaniah, Haggai, Zechariah, Malachi.

And the Writings:
- Psalms, Proverbs, Job, The Song of Solomon, Ruth, Lamentations, Ecclesiastes, Esther, Daniel, Ezra, Nehemiah, 1 and 2 Chronicles.

By 300 BC most of the Jews living outside of Palestine, or the Diaspora, were residing in the Greek-speaking world. The city of Alexandria held a large Greek-speaking Jewish community who could no longer understand their original scripture text. The legend is that Ptolemy II (309–246 BC), king of Egypt, commissioned seventy-two scholars in Alexandria to translate the Hebrew text of the Old Testament into Greek. Hence, its nickname, the Septuagint (or LXX, for the Roman numeral for seventy), refers to the seventy plus scholars who translated the text. This Greek version of the Hebrew Bible was used by Greek-speaking Jews during the time of Christ. Even in the cosmopolitan city of Jerusalem, it was widely used because many of the Jews there spoke Greek and Aramaic. This is illustrated by Josephus's use of the Septuagint (LXX) in his quoting of Jewish scripture and the many New Testament quotations of the Old Testament from the Septuagint not the Hebrew text.[6] For the Jews in Jerusalem and those living in the Hellenized world, the Septuagint version of the Torah became "really the people's Bible to that large Jewish world through which Christianity was afterwards to address itself to mankind."[7]

## SAYINGS AND TARGUMIM

Although Hebrew was not the language known or used by most of the Jews, for the rabbi or Jewish scholar the Hebrew version of scripture was still the religious authoritative text. As a result, during the intertestimental period (between the Old and New Testaments), knowledge of the Hebrew law began to hold a place of great importance in Jewish society and its interpretation would create a new level of scriptural writings for the Jewish people.

Students and teachers of theology enjoyed exceptional honor in the Jewish community of Jesus' day.[8] The rabbis were held in highest esteem because of their knowledge of the Hebrew law in every small respect. Their exalted position was due to their ability to read the Hebrew text, "figure out" the law, and teach it to others. The Old Testament taught, "Act according to the law they teach you and the decision they give you. Do not turn aside from what they tell you, to the right or to the left" (Deuteronomy 17:11, Edersheim's translation).[9] In reference to this scripture, a well-respected rabbi of the thirteenth century stated, "Even if a Rabbi were to teach that your left hand was the right, and your right hand the left, you are bound to obey."[10]

Jewish rabbis would discuss the meaning of the scriptures and their practical application in real-life situations. Many of these scriptural lessons were done in story form or as parables to teach people how to live the law. Originally, this was done through an oral tradition passed down from generation to generation, from teacher to student. These constituted the sayings of the scribes or the sayings of the Pharisees, about which Jesus said the Pharisees did "bind heavy burdens and grievous to be borne, and lay them on men's shoulders: but they themselves will not move them with one of their fingers" (Matthew 23:4).

A TARGUM IS A translation or simple paraphrase of Hebrew scripture in Aramaic, the spoken language of the common people at the time of Christ. These were given after public readings of the scriptures. The plural of *Targum* is *Targumim*.

The first scriptural commentaries used in the synagogue were called *Targumim*. Unlike the verbose and detailed sayings of the scribes, Targumim were translations or simple paraphrases of Hebrew scripture in the spoken language of the common people, Aramaic, given after public reading of the scriptures. The practice dated from before Jesus and continued through his life. These simple paraphrases gave the common Jews some idea of how they should interpret the Old Testament.

Elder Talmage made reference to the Targumim when he discussed Jesus' return to his boyhood home of Nazareth. He had come to the synagogue service on the Sabbath day. Growing up, Jesus sat in this same synagogue listening to the reading of the law and the Targumim by appointed readers. In the chapter note on this scriptural passage, Talmage cited Edersheim for further clarification on the use of these interpretations in the synagogue during Jesus' ministry: "Edersheim states that pure Hebrew was the language of scholars and of the synagogue, and that the public readings from the scriptures had to be rendered by an interpreter."[11] During the service, a translator was needed to "translate the portion of Scripture read in the public services and the addresses delivered by the Rabbis."[12]

Since Jesus was now of legal age and a teacher of some renown,  he was given the reader's place. He read in Isaiah 61:1–2 and was then allowed to offer a *Targum*, meaning to expound or give some commentary. The Savior's interpretation of this scripture was startling: "This day is this scripture fulfilled in your ears" (Luke 4:21). This remarkable saying was easily understood by all in the congregation. Yet many would not believe his words. All they could think was, "Is not this Joseph's son?" (Luke 4:22).

## MISHNAH AND TALMUD

After the destruction of the temple in AD 70, the Jewish people did not have a center of worship in their homeland. The scattered Jews were even more disconnected without a place to carry on the feasts and festivals. The temple had served as a place for scattered Israel to gather, teach, and discuss the gospel during these sacred times of the year. The need for these oral traditions to be written down became a necessity. Centuries after the Savior's ministry, the sayings of the rabbis and Jewish teachers were collected and compiled by various schools and rabbinical writers and became part of the authoritative religious teachings of the Jews.

DIASPORA LITERALLY
means "dispersion," and refers to the scattering
of Israel into other lands than Palestine.

The Mishnah, compiled about the second century AD, was primarily written by Jehudah the Holy and is one of the oldest of these traditional books. The Mishnah is the "great text-book of Rabbinism."[13] The purpose of the Mishnah is to be a "handbook of legal determination in their utmost logical sequences [and is] enlivened"[14] by stories told to illustrate some particular point of Jewish doctrine. There are six orders, each devoted to a class of subjects (religious-agrarian laws, feasts and festivals, women, damages, holy things, cleanliness). Each order is divided into tractates and verses.

Other authoritative compilations were later collected based on the original organization of the Mishnah. The Jerusalem Talmud (completed about AD 350–400) and the Babylonian Talmud (completed about AD 500) are other sacred Jewish writings based on these oral traditions of the rabbis that expound more broadly on the same subjects as the Mishnah. Edersheim delighted in reading the Talmud and Mishnah, finding in both of them "many sparkling, beautiful, and occasionally almost sublime passages."[15] Yet he is the first to admit that after reading even a part of the Talmud, there is no comparing "the Talmud with the New Testament."[16]

THE MISHNAH (AD 200),
the Jerusalem Talmud (AD 350–400), and the
Babylonian Talmud (AD 500) are compilations
of the oral traditions of the rabbis.

Edersheim does use many quotes and stories from the Talmud and Mishnah in his commentaries about Jewish life during the time of Christ and directly correlates the teachings of the Talmud and Mishnah, which were written hundreds of years after Christ's time. Many gospel scholars find this unscholarly and disagree with his assumptions that these Jewish stories and interpretations may still be applicable to this earlier time period. Although Edersheim's Talmud or Mishnah quotes are not necessarily from the same period, these oral traditions were an integral part of Jewish culture at that time. Many of the stories and teachings could not only have relevance, but may have originated hundreds of year before; however, it is very difficult to determine which ones do and which ones do not. In spite of these challenges, the Talmud and Mishnah can often shed additional light in understanding passages in both the Old and New Testament.

## STUDYING THE LAW

A rabbi told the story how he, as a young man, had been scandalized to see older rabbis running on the Sabbath to get to a sermon on time when such bodily exercise was usually forbidden. These older rabbis pointed out that in Hosea 11:10 the word of the Lord is described as a "roar like a lion" and when the Lord roars, we should run to hear it. This young rabbi was taught that part of the reward of devotion, scripture reading, and scholarly discourse is the haste with which people run to do it.[17] Soon, he joined the rest of the rabbis in their race to hear the word of the Lord.

The Jews believed they should hasten in their devotions to the Lord, which combined scripture study with prayer, temple worship, and services at the local synagogue. This attitude was supported by the prophet Hosea's words, "Then shall we know, if we follow on to know the Lord" (Hosea 6:3). Edersheim pointed out a better translation for this verse might be: "Let us pursue to know the Lord."[18] Thus, according to biblical text our religious devotions should not be done in a slow or lazy way.

In the Talmud, the direction is given to leave the synagogue with slow steps but "hasten to it as rapidly as possible."[19] The study of the sacred words of God was a part of almost every Jewish boy's early life.

At the destruction of Jerusalem, there was estimated to be no fewer than 480 schools in the city limits of Jerusalem.[20] The object of their lessons was moral and intellectual training through study of the Torah. The holy calling of the teacher was to fill the children's minds "with thoughts of God specially sacred."[21] The Bible was studied in the order of importance, with first the Law, then the Prophets, and finally the Writings.

## THE BOY JESUS IN THE TEMPLE—
## A SPIRITUAL AWAKENING

Edersheim supposed that in Joseph and Mary's home, the boy Jesus was taught from the Hebrew text of the scriptures. He makes an intriguing argument for Jesus' use and study of the Hebrew version of the Old Testament, not the Septuagint: "Only an appeal to the Hebrew Scriptures could have been of authority in discussion with the Pharisees and Scribes, and that it alone gave point to the frequent expostulations of Christ, 'Have ye not read?' "[22] The young boy was so familiar with the entire sacred volume that the scriptures must have been the "meat and drink of the God-Man."[23] He would have been taught by his stepfather, Joseph, to read and study them. Edersheim supposed that Christ's own forgotten memory might have been stirred as he read his own words. He would have gone to a synagogue school and learned with the other boys in Nazareth the scripture text. His familiarity from his earliest childhood with the Hebrew scripture explains how at age twelve Jesus was found "in the Temple, sitting in the midst of the doctors, both hearing them and asking them questions" (Luke 2:46).

Edersheim clarifies a common misconception that the reason Jesus came to the temple at the age of twelve was for a bar mitzvah. Bar mitzvah literally means "son of the commandment." At age thirteen, boys are now responsible under the law, and this change is celebrated by the family. The rabbinical law also directed boys at least one year before becoming a "son of the commandment"[24] to come to the temple and observe the Passover rites. This would have been the reason for Jesus coming to the temple for the first time at the age of twelve.

"HOW IS IT THAT YE sought me? Wist ye not that I must be about my Father's business?" (Luke 2:49)

During the Passover feast days, the members of the Sanhedrin would come out on the terrace of the temple and publicly teach and expound, allowing public questions and discussions on points of doctrine. These discussions would usually happen during the minor days of the festival, between the second and last day of the Paschal week. This is the same time Joseph and Mary were allowed, by Jewish law, to return home to Nazareth. Edersheim concludes that "these circumstances also explain why His appearance in the midst of the doctors, although very remarkable considering His age, did not at once command universal attention." Still, as Luke records, "And all that heard him were astonished at his understanding and answers" (2:47).

Edersheim speculates that Jesus' experience at the temple expounding scripture with the Pharisees and scribes was a spiritually awakening moment for him. His sense of mission was realized along with a greater understanding of who he really was.[25] However this awakening thought was kindled, he had become so entirely absorbed by it that he was neglectful and forgetful of all around him. Because of this encompassing feeling, it seemed to him impossible to understand how his parents could have sought him and not known why or where he had lingered. "And when they saw him, they were amazed: and his mother said unto him, Son, why hast thou thus dealt with us? Behold, thy father and I have sought thee sorrowing. And he said unto them, How is it that ye sought me? Wist ye not that I must be about my Father's business?" (Luke 2:48–49).

This awakening feeling made him realize the temple was emphatically his house. He felt comfortable there. He also felt a strong divine impulse and necessity of his being "about His Father's business" for maybe the first time in his young life. Edersheim continues, "That forgetfulness of His Child-life was a sacrifice—a sacrifice of self; that

*Key*

entire absorption in His Father's business, without a thought of self, either in the gratification of curiosity, the acquisition of knowledge, or personal ambition—a consecration of Himself unto God. It was the first manifestation of His passive and active obedience to the Will of God."[26]

Edersheim concludes with a wonderful "we" statement at the end of this discussion, "We all, when first awakening to spiritual consciousness . . . should make this the hour of decision, in which heart and life shall be wholly consecrated to the business of our Father."[27] This awakening to spiritual consciousness is something that can happen to all readers of the scriptures who study and worship God. Each reader can gain a greater understanding of his life's mission and who he really is.

## THE STRUGGLE OF THE SOUL

In the Talmud there is a story told about Elijah appearing in the form of an Arab merchant. He found a man praying with his face turned away from the synagogue. Elijah railed against the man, "Thou standest before thy Master as if there were two Powers (or Gods)."[28] For Jews, even outward signs of sacred worship should acknowledge service to God first and foremost. Whenever pious Jews prayed, even behind a synagogue, they would face that sacred building to demonstrate that the Lord was the focus of their devotions. This story is a graphic reminder of the importance of "putt[ing] off the natural man and becom[ing] a saint" (Mosiah 3:19).

A major purpose of the scriptures is to train our hearts and our minds to become Christ-centered rather than Mammon-centered: "No man can serve two masters: for either he will hate the one, and love the other; or else he will hold to the one, and despise the other. Ye cannot serve God and mammon" (Matthew 6:24). Scripture reading can redirect our natures so we can become more "submissive, meek, humble, patient, [and] full of love."[29]

Edersheim reminds us that from the beginning of this earth, there has been a pull between God and Mammon. There will ever be a conflict between humanity and the principles of evil, as represented by the serpent in the Garden of Eden. Even though we may still experience pain and the poison of death, through the scriptures we learn that humanity will ultimately be victorious because of our

Deliverer. This promise changes the context of our earth life: "It sets forth a principle; it ennobles our human nature by representing it as moral; it bears a promise; it contains a prophecy. . . . It is the noblest saying that could be given to Humanity, or to individual men, at the birth of their history."[30]

The Bible sets forth in its very opening the "three great ethical principles"[31] on which rest all scripture teachings concerning the Messiah and his kingdom:

1. Man is capable of salvation.
2. All evil springs from sin, with which mortal combat must be waged.
3. There will be a final victory over sin through the "Representative of Humanity."[32]

Each of these "ethical principles" rests on a single foundation, that of the critical role of a Messiah for the redemption of humankind. Edersheim recognized that all scripture, Old and New Testament combined, teaches of Jesus Christ and testifies of him and his mission on this earth. The Savior taught, "Search the scriptures . . . they are they which testify of me" (John 5:39).

## SCRIPTURAL CRITICISM

Edersheim's love of the scriptures caused him to study all subject areas. He studied languages, a variety of books and archaeological artifacts—all to the end of understanding the scriptures better. His scholarly pursuit "embodies the results of many years' study, in which I have availed myself of every help within my reach. It might seem affectation, were I to enumerate the names of all the authorities consulted or books read in the course of these studies."[33] Edersheim did not use his scriptural knowledge to tear down or question the truth of the scriptures. Instead, he believed in using scriptural commentary to clarify accurately a fuller view of scriptural truth.

In the never-ending conflict between truth and error, he was looking for "peaceful fruits"[34] as the ultimate gain from such scriptural discussions. His goal for theological writings and pursuits was "not that full and free criticism may be suppressed, but that it may be utilized, that so on the evening of the battle there may be assured peace, and the golden light shine around the old truth in her new garments of conquest, revealing the full perfection of her beauty."[35] His books were written to uplift others, enlighten minds with truth, and strengthen testimonies of the Savior, Jesus Christ.

> "ADMITTEDLY, HE WAS THE ONE perfect Man—the ideal of humanity; His doctrine the one absolute teaching. The world has known none other, none equal."—Alfred Edersheim

Yet Edersheim wrote during a time when scriptural criticism was just at its threshold. Many of these critics were questioning the Mosaic authorship of the Torah. The first systematic attempt to trace different documents written by different authors in the book of Genesis (and Exodus chapters 1 and 2) was made by Jean Astruc (1684–1766), a French physician and son of a Protestant pastor, and afterwards a convert to Roman Catholicism. He noted at least thirteen different documents in Genesis.[36] Edersheim pointed out that Martin Luther, in his book *Table-Talk*, implies the possibility of doubt, yet the unimportance of the question of Mosaic authorship. Other earlier writers came to similar conclusions (A. Masius, Hobbes, Spinoza, Simon, and Le Clerc).

Others were questioning the divine nature of the Mosaic law in general. Edersheim refuted these claims. He felt that such overanalyzing of the Bible "takes away all the sacred elements, and Israel appears as only a horde of barbarians and of slaves."[37] Biblical criticism and science, which has as its sole purpose the destruction of the history and sacred legislation of the Old Testament, will not be able to shake "from their hinges those 'everlasting doors' by which Christ the King of Glory has entered in. . . . For Christ has come: the reality of all types, the fulfillment of all promises, the Son of David, the Saviour of the world."[38]

Edersheim was hopeful that scripture study would strengthen the testimonies of all who regularly enjoy reading the words of God. He was happy to see people during his day have an increased awareness and interest in the Bible. He felt sure that such investigations into the Bible would only prove its truthfulness and increase people's testimonies of Christ. He wrote, "One of the most marked and hopeful signs of our time is the increasing attention given on all sides to the study of Holy Scripture. Those who believe and love the Bible, who have experienced its truth and power, can only rejoice at such an issue. . . . For the more the Bible is studied the deeper will be our conviction that the foundation of God standeth sure."[39]

## EDERSHEIM AND RESTORED SCRIPTURAL TRUTH

Edersheim, of course, did not have access to restored truth or modern scriptures. He did sense incompleteness in the theology of his religion, recognizing knowledge lacking in the Christianity he knew. Searching for a "universal" Christian church, Edersheim chose to leave the original Christian church in which he was baptized to join the most universal Christian church in England, the Anglican Church. Even after this change, though, he realized there were many theological questions left unanswered. He expressed concern about preachers who are "in the habit of asking a series of questions from the pulpit when they immediately add: These are questions which we cannot answer."[40]

Edersheim acknowledged that these many unanswered questions were the basis for much of the contentions of his day. Edersheim pointed out, "Our religious differences mostly spring from what all of us do not know, but pretend to know."[41] He recognized that there were parts of gospel truth unavailable to him, though his study of the Bible and his feasting on the words of Christ gave him many scriptural insights.

With the restoration of The Church of Jesus Christ of Latter-day Saints in its fulness, many of those questions have been answered through modern revelation, expanding the body of revealed truth. President Joseph Fielding Smith reminded members that modern revelation, as put forth in newly revealed scripture and the words of living prophets, are for all the world, but those who have taken on Christ's name will be judged by them, whether they read them or not: "We will all be judged by it, by the things which the other books contain which are holy scripture, which the Lord has given unto us; and if we fail to comprehend these things, if we will not search, if we will not study, if we will not take hold on the things which the Lord has revealed unto us, then his condemnation shall rest upon us."[42]

Edersheim's love for the scriptures and revealed truth is a great example for us today. In writing his scriptural commentaries, he was hoping "to help, so far as we can, the reader of Holy Scripture—not to supersede his own reading of it."[43] Similarly, it is hoped that this reference book will encourage the reader to study the scriptures and words of our Holy Prophets today more diligently, rather than be a substitute for it.

# NOTES

1. Edersheim, *Sketches*, 118. This story is from the Talmud (*Men.* 99 b).
2. Edersheim, *Sketches*, 118.
3. Edersheim, *Sketches*, 117.
4. Edersheim, *Sketches*, 117.
5. Edersheim, *Bible History*, 9.
6. Edersheim, *Jesus the Messiah*, 12–21 (1:18–30). For further information, read book 1 chapter 2, entitled "The Jewish dispersion in the West—The Hellenists—Origin of the Hellenist Literature in the Greek Translation of the Bible—Character of the Septuagint."
7. Edersheim, *Jesus the Messiah*, 20 (1:29).
8. See Matthew 23:6–7; Mark 12:38–39; Luke 11:43.
9. Edersheim, *Sketches*, 120.
10. Edersheim, *Sketches*, 120.
11. Talmage, *Jesus the Christ*, chapter 13, note 4, 186.
12. Talmage, *Jesus the Christ*, chapter 13, note 4, 186.
13. Edersheim, *Sketches*, 67.
14. Edersheim, *Sketches*, 67.
15. Edersheim, *Jesus the Messiah*, 72 (1:105).
16. Edersheim, *Jesus the Messiah*, 73 (1:106). For further reading on the subject, read in book 1 chapter 8 entitled, "Traditionalism, its origin, character, and literature—The Mishnah and Talmud—The Gospel of Christ—The dawn of a new day."
17. Edersheim, *Sketches*, 238. "And so Rabbi Seira, as it seems to us, somewhat caustically concludes: 'The reward of a discourse is the haste' with which people run to it—no matter, it would appear, whether they get in to hear it, or whether there is anything in the discourse worth the hearing."

18. Edersheim, *Sketches*, 237.

19. Edersheim, *Sketches*, 237.

20. Edersheim, *Sketches*, 126.

21. Edersheim, *Sketches*, 126.

22. Edersheim, *Sketches*, 112. See Matthew 12:3; 19:4; 21:13, 16, 42; 22:31.

23. Edersheim, *Sketches*, 111.

24. Edersheim, *Sketches*, 113.

25. Edersheim, *Jesus the Messiah*, 167–73 (1:240–51). This is a complete description of this wonderful experience.

26. Edersheim, *Jesus the Messiah*, 172–73 (1:250).

27. Edersheim, *Jesus the Messiah*, 172 (1:249).

28. Edersheim, *Sketches*, 236.

29. Mosiah 3:19—The beginning of this verse reads, "For the natural man is an enemy to God and has been from the fall of Adam, and will be forever and ever, unless he yields to the enticings of the Holy Spirit."

30. Edersheim, *Lectures*, 34.

31. Edersheim, *Lectures*, 34.

32. Edersheim, *Lectures*, 34.

33. Edersheim, *Sketches*, viii.

34. Edersheim, *Lectures*, viii.

35. Edersheim, *Lectures*, ix.

36. Edersheim, *Lectures*, 192–93.

37. Edersheim, *Lectures*, 227.

38. Edersheim, *Lectures*, 228–29.

39. Edersheim, *Bible History*, 3.

40. Edersheim, *Bible History*, 83.

41. Edersheim, *Bible History*, 104.

42. Joseph Fielding Smith, CR, Oct. 1919, 146.

43. Edersheim, *Bible History*, 3.

# CHAPTER SIX

# JEWISH FAMILY LIFE

OF ALL HIS CREATIONS, God created only man "in [his] own image" (Moses 2:27). In his *Bible History* Edersheim expressed the concept that this scripture refers not only to the physical characteristics and intelligence God endowed to him, but also the "perfect moral and spiritual nature"[1] man first possessed in the Garden of Eden. All his surroundings in the garden were in accordance with his happy state. God "put him into the garden of Eden to dress it and to keep it" (Genesis 2:15) and gave him a companion in Eve, whom Adam realized was "bone of my bones, and flesh of my flesh" (Genesis 2:23). In the garden, God also set apart the Sabbath day, indicating the need for a day of rest from man's worldly labors: "And God blessed the seventh day, and sanctified it: because that in it he had rested from all his work which God created and made" (Genesis 2:3).

So, God laid in paradise the foundation of civil society, a threefold foundation of family, work, and worship. First, he provided man with an arena in which to focus his efforts. Then, he instituted marriage and the family. He also laid the foundation of the proper relationship between man and his Creator through the institution of Sabbath worship and prayer.[2] This thought of Edersheim is echoed in "The Family: A Proclamation to the World": "The family is ordained of God.

Marriage between man and woman is essential to His eternal plan. . . . Successful marriages and families are established and maintained on principles of faith, prayer, repentance, forgiveness, respect, love, compassion, work, and wholesome recreational activities."[3]

The Jewish home practiced and taught the importance of loving family relationships. It was a place of work and worship where children were taught to love God and follow his commandments. The fifth commandment given to Moses was "Honour thy father and thy mother" (Exodus 20:12). The Jews took this commandment very seriously. They also took seriously the words of Jehovah, "I am the Lord thy God" (Exodus 20:2). Their devotions to Jehovah were taken from the law, and they followed them even in the privacy of their homes.

## FAMILY RELATIONSHIPS

There is a tender bond that unites Jewish parents to their children. This is illustrated in the multiple Hebrew terms used to depict the different stages of the developing child. Of course, there are the general terms of son (ben) and daughter (bath). But the English term baby is delineated by the Jews into five stages: newborn (jeled), the nursing baby (jonek), the baby that needs additional nourishment but is still nursing (olel), the weaned baby (gamul), and finally, the toddler or young child still clinging to its mother (taph).[4] The Jews are keenly aware of the child-life stages and are fondly attached to their children. From the scriptures, we are taught that "sons are a heritage of the Lord," and that children are a reward from him (Psalm 127:3).

Just as parents are to take tender care of their young children, children should also honor their mother and father and care for them in their old age. A rabbinical saying taught, "Just as the pieces of the broken tables of the law were kept in the ark, so old age should be venerated and cherished, even though it should be broken in mind or memory."[5]

No commandment was more severely punished by the Jews than a breach of the fifth commandment. If a son was stubborn and rebellious and would not obey the voice of his mother and father, Jewish law allowed his parents to take him before the elders of his city and witness against him "and all the men of his city shall stone him with stones, that he die" (Deuteronomy 21:21). The Levites cursed sons and daughters who esteemed lightly or disgraced their father or mother.[6]

CORBAN MEANS A GIFT
given to God. By declaring their possessions
*corban*, the Jews kept personal use of their
possessions, but they ironically did not need
to share them with other specified persons.
Thus, they were freed from their sacred family
responsibilities of helping an aged parent or a
needy sibling.

Yet, during the time of the Savior, Jewish children would try to get out of taking care of their parents by declaring their goods to be *corban*,[7] or a gift[8] given to God. Edersheim made the distinction: "It must not be thought that pronunciation of the votive word *Corban* . . . necessarily dedicated a thing to the Temple. The meaning might simply be, and generally was, that it was to be regarded like *Corban*—that is, that in regard to the person or persons named, the thing termed was to be considered as if it were *Corban*, lain on the altar, and put entirely out of their reach."[9] The binding of this vow was greater than their responsibility to help their parents. By declaring their possessions corban, they kept their own use of their possessions, but did not need to share them with other specified persons. Thus, they were freed from their sacred family responsibilities of helping an aged parent or a needy sibling.

The Savior rebuked those who did this practice as "making the word of God of none effect through your tradition" (Mark 7:13). Christ was illustrating the hypocrisy of the system of traditionalism, which connected an outward meticulous observance to the law with a gross violation of duty. The law was not supposed to be a system of external, outward things affecting the inner man. Instead, the law was supposed to spring from moral action within. Moral principles of his gospel were "not from without inwards, but from within outwards."[10] This was the principle for his new kingdom and the law in its fulness.

The greatest example we have of the tender feelings that should exist in a family is given to us by our Heavenly Father. God presented himself to man, as their Father. This example would give "peculiar strength and sacredness to the bond which connected earthly parents with their offspring."[11] Through latter-day revelation, we know that each one of us "is a beloved spirit son or daughter of heavenly parents"[12] and "the family is central to the Creator's plan for the eternal destiny of His children."[13]

## THE SHEMA AND PHYLACTERIES

Religion permeated the daily life of the Jewish family. The law of the Lord was to be taught diligently in Jewish homes so that the commandments were written in their hearts every hour of the day: "And these words, which I command thee this day, shall be in thine heart: And thou shalt teach them diligently unto thy children, and shalt talk of them when thou sittest in thine house, and when thou walkest by the way, and when thou liest down, and when thou risest up" (Deuteronomy 6:6–7). This excerpt comes from the Shema which is comprised of three passages of scripture[14] (Deuteronomy 6:4–9; 11:13–21; and Numbers 15:37–41). These three passages make up a creed or statement of belief for the Jewish people. The name Shema comes from the Hebrew translation of the first word of Deuteronomy 6:4: "Hear, O Israel." These scriptures form part of the regular daily prayers of the Jewish people in their homes and in the synagogue.

These passages were taken very literally by the children of Israel. In Deuteronomy 6:9, the Lord commands the children of Israel, "And thou shalt write them upon the posts of thy house, and on thy gates." The interpretation of this scripture was the mezuzah (discussed earlier), which was a small cylinder attached to the side of the house containing two scriptures (Deuteronomy 6:9; 11:20).[15] The family members would reverently touch the mezuzah and afterwards kiss their finger, speaking at the same time a quiet benediction. This would provide divine protection for the family: "The Lord shall preserve thy going out and thy coming in from this time forth, and even for evermore" (Psalm 121:8). It also served as a perpetual learning moment for children as they saw older family members performing this quick ritual many times a day.

THE CAPSULES OR SMALL boxes were fastened on by black leather straps, which were wound around the arm (seven times) and hand (three times) or else fitted to the forehead in a prescribed and mystically significant manner.

Another literal Jewish interpretation of the Shema came from Deuteronomy 6:8: "And thou shalt bind them for a sign upon thine hands, and they shall be as frontlets between thine eyes."[16] Because of this scriptural passage, the Jews, especially during the time of Christ, wore phylacteries on the head and arm. An ordinary pious Jew would only put them on during prayer or solemn occasions, but the Pharisees would wear them all day long. The tephillin, or phylacteries, were worn on the left arm toward the heart and on the forehead. Edersheim described them as "capsules, containing on parchment (that for the forehead on four distinct parchments), these four passages of scripture: Exodus 13:1–10; 13:11–16; Deuteronomy 6:4–9; and 11:13–21."[17]

The capsules or small boxes were fastened on by black leather straps, which were wound around the arm (seven times) and hand (three times) or else fitted to the forehead in a prescribed and mystically significant manner. The wearer of them could not be mistaken.[18] Edersheim described their importance in the eyes of the rabbis. Tephillin could be rescued from flames on the Sabbath, and wearing them did not constitute a burden. The tephillin were more sacred than the golden plate worn by the high priest because they contained the name of Jehovah twenty-three times, while the golden band only has it once. The Jews supposed that even God himself wore phylacteries.[19]

DURING THE TIME OF THE Savior, the Pharisees would make a big show of these outward signs of devotion.

During the time of the Savior, the Pharisees would make a big show of these outward signs of devotion. They made their phylacteries large so they were easily seen, and they enlarged the borders of their tallith or their square blue and white fringed garments for show. Jesus warned the Pharisees that such traditions would not save them: "Howbeit in vain do they worship me, teaching for doctrines the commandments of men. For laying aside the commandment of God, ye hold the tradition of men, as the washing of pots and cups: and many other such like things ye do" (Mark 7:7–8).

## SABBATH WORSHIP

In the pious Jewish home, the labor of every week was sanctified by the return of the Sabbath:

> As the head of the house returned on the Sabbath eve from the synagogue to his home, he found it festively adorned, the Sabbath lamp brightly burning, and the table spread with the richest each household could afford. But first he blessed each child with the blessing of Israel. And next evening, when the Sabbath light faded out, he made solemn separation between the hallowed day and the working week, and so commenced his labor once more in the name of the Lord.[20]

The Sabbath was welcomed into the home as a king or a bridegroom, and it was observed as a day of rest and joy. The stranger, the widow, the poor, and the fatherless were not forgotten on the Sabbath. All were cared for on this Holy Day. The Sabbath was to be a delight. The day was to be honored and all were to find pleasure in it.

By the time of the Savior, there was an inordinate amount of rules about what constituted "labor" and what Jews could and could not do on the Sabbath in order to keep the day a day of rest. The fundamental idea of the sacred Sabbath still remained, but the rabbis held "terribly exaggerated views"[21] on Sabbath day observance, which had become a burden to many.

The Pharisees often battled with Jesus over Sabbath day observances. They watched him to see if he would heal on the Sabbath so they could accuse him of breaking one of the many Sabbath rules. Jesus perceived their thoughts and asked them, "Is it lawful on the Sabbath days to do good, or to do evil? To save life, or to destroy it?" (Luke 6:9).

He brought forward a man with a withered hand and had him stretch forth his hand. His hand was miraculously restored. "The Savior had broken their Sabbath-Law, and yet He had not broken it, for neither by remedy, nor touch, nor outward application had he healed him. He had broken the Sabbath-rest, as God breaks it, when He sends, or sustains, or restores life or does good; all unseen and unheard, without touch our outward application, by the Word of His Power, by the Presence of His Life."[22] As the Pharisees saw this act of creation, "They were filled with madness" (Luke 6:11). They were too burdened by their own misunderstanding of the Sabbath to feel the delight of this Sabbath-day miracle.

## THE TREATMENT OF WOMEN

There was a Jewish ideal for the relationships between man and wife, children and parents, the young and the aged. Within this ideal, women were treated with respect and given more legal rights in the Jewish community than the women of neighboring countries or regions conquered by the Romans. Even the Hebrew name for woman, given her at creation (Genesis 2:23), denotes a wife as the companion of her husband, and his equal—*Ishah*, a woman, from *Ish*, a man.[23] The creation of woman from the rib of man is commented on in the Talmud: "It is as if Adam had exchanged a pot of earth for a precious jewel."[24] A Jewish woman is viewed as a valuable partner in the home, giving spiritual insight and wisdom to her family. There is a Jewish legend that says the women of Israel contributed of their substance to build the Tabernacle, but they refused to give of their goods to make the golden calf.[25]

A Jewish woman during the time of Christ did have some legal rights under the law. At the time of her betrothal, a woman was treated as if she were married. The betrothal was marked by a bridal present or *Mohar* (Genesis 34:12; Exodus 22:17). To make the betrothal legally valid, a piece of money was given directly to the woman and witnessed that the man intended to espouse the woman as his wife. At this point, the union was legally binding and could not be absolved except by a regular divorce.

The marriage would follow later, often after as long as a year of waiting. At her wedding, the bride's father was to provide a dowry, which really belonged to the wife. She was entitled to one-tenth of her dowry for pin money at the time of her marriage. Even an orphan girl without a dowry was allowed to receive fifty sus from the town authorities.[26] For the most part, all property was owned by the husband. The dowry money became the woman's at the death of her husband, but he was able to use her money and property as he saw fit. The only exception was the *mohar,* or the bride gift, and the tenth of her dowry money. These were hers to always keep.

The marriage customs in Judea required appointing a chief groomsman, who would take care of all the arrangements for the wedding feast. He was known as "the friend of the bridegroom" (John 3:29). In contrast, in Galilee, a "friend of the bridegroom" was not often chosen. Instead the expression "children of the bridechamber" (Matthew 9:15; Mark 2:19; Luke 5:34) was used to mean all the invited guests to the wedding. Edersheim wrote, "As the institution of 'friends of the bridegroom' prevailed in Judea, but not in Galilee, this marked distinction of the 'friend of the bridegroom' in the mouth of the Judean John, and 'sons (children) of the bridechamber' in that of the Galilean Jesus, is itself evidential of historic accuracy."[27]

The parable of the ten virgins was also taken from this Jewish tradition of waiting expectantly for the bridegroom (Matthew 25:1). It was an Eastern custom that when the bride was led to her future home, ten lamps were carried before the party.[28]

The Talmud counsels husbands on how to treat their wives. This is very similar to Paul's counsel in Ephesians 5:28. The Talmud reads, "He that loveth his wife as his own body, honoureth her more than his own body, brings up his children in the right way, and leads them in it to full age—of him the scripture saith: 'Thou shalt know that thy tabernacle shall be in peace' (Job 5:24)."[29] Jewish women were expected to show forth qualities of "meekness, modesty, and shamefacedness."[30] Indeed, immodest behaviors in public (gossiping, brawling in the streets) were sufficient grounds for divorce. Jewish women would never attempt to teach in the synagogue. They were separated from men during worship services and were not to usurp man's authority in the teaching of the law.[31]

By the time of the Savior, it was easy for a man to divorce his wife, and it seems to have been done quite frequently. The Pharisees asked the Savior, "Is it lawful for a man to put away his wife for every cause?" (Matthew 19:3). Edersheim proposed that a better reading of this question might be "for every offence."[32] A letter of divorce was handed to the woman herself in the presence of two witnesses, and that was all that was needed to terminate the marriage. The Savior realized the hypocrisy of this tradition and used the Hebrew scriptures to answer their question: "Have ye not read, that he which made them at the beginning made them male and female. . . . Wherefore they are no more twain, but one flesh. What therefore God hath joined together, let not man put asunder" (Matthew 19:4, 6).

Girls were not given the same amount of education and instruction in the law and scriptures as boys were, even though they were allowed and often encouraged to attend elementary schools and learn to read and write. It was not approved for girls to engage in legal studies since their duties were in caring for the home and family. The saying was that "women are of a light mind"[33] and unable to fathom the logical legal intricacies of the law. However, there are scriptural instances of women learned in the law, like Deborah, who was a judge in Israel (Judges 4:4–5), and Huldah, the prophetess who interpreted the law for King Josiah (2 Kings 22:14; 2 Chronicles 34:22). In the New Testament, there were women who knew the law well enough to teach it to their sons, even without a Jewish father in the home, such as the case of Timothy.

## TIMOTHY—A GOOD JEWISH BOY

It was the responsibility of Jewish parents to make sure their children were taught the ways of the Lord. As early as five years old, Jewish children were supposed to start reading the Bible. At the age of six or seven, Jewish parents were legally bound to attend to the formal schooling of their children. In the New Testament, there is the story of Eunice, the daughter of pious Lois and the mother of Timothy. She felt the responsibility most Jewish parents feel to teach their children the commandments of God, but she had many obstacles in her way. Eunice married a Greek and lived in the city of Lystra, where there were no Jewish synagogues and very few Jews. Despite these difficulties, Lois and Eunice made sure that Timothy was taught from the time he was a *taph*, a child still clinging to his mother, to have faith in the Jewish scriptures. Paul commented on Timothy's scriptural knowledge, "From a child thou hast known the holy scriptures" (2 Timothy 3:15). Regarding Timothy's faith, Paul noted, "I call to remembrance the unfeigned faith that is in thee, which dwelt first in thy grandmother Lois, and thy mother, Eunice" (2 Timothy 1:5). In the life of Timothy, a good Jewish boy, these women were "the one influence for highest good—constant unvarying and most powerful."[34]

## PRAYER AND FRINGED GARMENTS

Because the home was the center of religious teaching and worship, prayer at home was done individually and as a family. There is a beautiful rabbinic saying: "He who prays in his house surrounds and fortifies it, so to speak, with a wall of iron."[35] Private prayers, morning and evening family prayers, and family religious practices hallowed daily life and pervaded the home.[36]

A special custom was to teach a child a verse of scripture that began and ended with precisely the same letters as his Hebrew name. The child would insert it into his daily prayers, and this birthday scripture became a "guardian-promise" for the child. These words would become familiar to his mind and "would remain with the youth in life's temptations, and come back amid the din of manhood's battle."[37]

As another physical reminder to always remember the Lord, the men would wear fringes on the border, or hem, of their outer garments (Numbers 15:38; Deuteronomy 22:12). In scripture, these fringes were to be of blue, the symbolic color of the covenant, but the Mishnah allowed them to be white also.[38] This square outer garment, or tallith, would have the customary fringes of four long white threads, with one of hyacinth knotted together on each of the four corners. The Pharisees would make these garments particularly wide so as to attract attention.[39] Jesus also wore them, as illustrated by the scriptures describing the sick who wanting to touch the border, hem, or fringe of his garment in order to be made whole.[40]

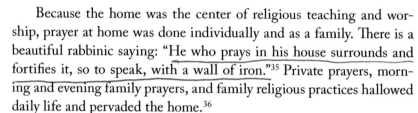

AS A PHYSICAL REMINDER to always remember the Lord, the men would wear fringes on the border (or hem) of their outer garments (Numbers 15:37; Deuteronomy 22:12).

# THE WOMAN WITH AN ISSUE OF BLOOD

Jairus, one of the synagogue rulers of Capernaum, had an only daughter. He loved her very much, and she was at the point of death. In his hour of extreme need, he went to Jesus, falling down at his feet, "and besought him that he would come into his house" (Luke 8:41). The Savior followed him to his home, pushing through a throng of people.

A woman with an issue of blood for twelve years was in the multitude. She had "spent all her living upon physicians, neither could be healed of any" (Luke 8:43). According to Jewish custom, she would have been unclean and would have defiled anyone and anything she touched. She would have been ostracized from her family, loved ones, and society in general. Yet, after touching the Savior, she was made clean once more. Edersheim described the faith of this woman: "What strong faith to expect help where all human help, so long and earnestly sought, had so signally failed! And what strong faith to expect, that even contact with Him, the bare touch of His garment, would carry such Divine Power as to make her whole. She put forth her hand and 'touched the border of His garment' most probably one of the corners of the Tallith."[41]

"SHE PUT FORTH her hand and 'touched the border of His garment' most probably one of the corners of the Tallith."— Alfred Edersheim

After touching the border of the Savior's garment, "immediately her issue of blood stanched" (Luke 8:44). Many had touched him in the throng, but it was only her faith that caused Jesus to say, "Virtue is gone out of me" (Luke 8:46). Hers was a real touch or connection because of her faith. Edersheim added a comment directed at "us" to also become connected with our Savior: "While even one real touch, if it were only of His garment, one real act of contact, however mediate, would bring us perfect healing. And in some sense it really is so. For, assuredly, the Lord cannot be touched by disease and misery, without healing coming from Him."[42]

Interestingly, Edersheim listed some of the different remedies for the flux in the Talmud: a combination of tonics and superstition. Two unusual cures listed are carrying the ashes of an ostrich-egg in summer in a linen rag and carrying a barley-corn found in the dung of a white she-ass.[43] He also pointed out that while the woman took these medications she was to be addressed in the words, "Arise, (*qum*) from the flux."[44] The Savior would use the same word, *qum*, in raising the daughter of Jairus from the dead. But he would not need to tell this woman to "arise," for her faith had healed her.

When Jesus turned, searching for the woman, she realized she would be found and came out trembling. "Falling down before him, she declared unto him before all the people for what cause she had touched him, and how she was healed immediately. And he said unto her, Daughter, be of good comfort: thy faith hath made thee whole; go in peace" (Luke 8:47–48). Edersheim felt one of the reasons the Savior sought the woman was to teach her that it was he who healed her, not his garment. He did not want her faith to be based on the garment itself, but in him: "Such excess might degenerate into superstition. . . . Not the garments in which He appeared among men, and which touched His Sacred Body, nor even that Body, but Himself brings healing. Again, there was the danger of losing sight of that which, as the moral element, is necessary in faith: personal application to, and personal contact with, Christ."[45]

While this miracle was occurring, Jairus's daughter had passed from this life. The Savior told Jairus, "Fear not: believe only, and she shall be made whole" (Luke 8:50). Jairus had to exercise faith that his family could be reunited once more. As Jesus came to Jairus's home, he put out the mourners and brought Jairus, his wife, and three Apostles into the daughter's chamber. He spoke two words: "Talyetha, Qum!" or "Maid, arise!" and "her spirit came again, and she arose straightway" (Luke 8:54–55). The parents were reunited once more with their daughter. The beauty of this story is the hope it brings to all families of the Savior's power to reunite them together again without the fear of death. The Savior is he "who hath abolished death, and hath brought life and immortality to light through the gospel" (2 Timothy 1:10).

As Edersheim expressed, this belief represents "our dearest hopes for ourselves and those we love."[46]

## NOTES

1. Edersheim, *Bible History*, 13.
2. Edersheim, *Bible History*, 13. Read pp. 13–17 for additional thoughts on the Garden of Eden.
3. "The Family: A Proclamation to the World," *Ensign*, Nov. 1995, 102.
4. Edersheim, *Sketches*, 99–100.
5. Edersheim, *Sketches*, 97.
6. Deuteronomy 27:16. See the footnote for "setteth light."
7. See Bible Dictionary, "corban," 650.
8. Matthew 15:5 calls it a gift.
9. Edersheim, *Jesus the Messiah*, 488–89 (2:20–22).
10. Edersheim, *Jesus the Messiah*, 489 (2:22).
11. Edersheim, *Sketches*, 95.
12. "The Family: A Proclamation to the World," *Ensign*, Nov. 1995, 102.
13. "The Family: A Proclamation to the World," *Ensign*, Nov. 1995, 102.
14. Edersheim, *Sketches*, 111, 245.
15. Edersheim, *Sketches*, 102–3. The mezuzah was only affixed on dwellings of honor and homes, not to bathrooms, wash houses, tanneries, dyeworks, nor even synagogues (see note 2 on p. 102).
16. Other similar scriptures are Exodus 13:9; Proverbs 3:3; 6:21; 7:3; and Isaiah 49:16.
17. Edersheim, *Sketches*, 203–4.
18. Edersheim, *Sketches*, 203–4.
19. Edersheim, *Sketches*, 203–4.
20. Edersheim, *Sketches*, 94.
21. Edersheim, *Jesus the Messiah*, 510 (2:53).
22. Edersheim, *Jesus the Messiah*, 512 (2:62).
23. Edersheim, *Sketches*, 95.
24. Edersheim, *Sketches*, 130.
25. Edersheim, *Sketches*, 130, note 3.
26. Edersheim, *Sketches*, 138–39.
27. Edersheim, quoted in Talmage, *Jesus the Christ* (1983), chapter 12, note 10, 160.
28. Edersheim, *Sketches*, 143, note 112.
29. Edersheim, *Sketches*, 135. The Talmud reference is *Yeb. 62b, Sanh. 76b.*
30. Edersheim, *Sketches*, 135.
31. Edersheim, *Sketches*, 135. See Paul's counsel on this in 1 Timothy 2:12.

32. Edersheim, *Sketches*, 114, note 13.

33. Edersheim, *Sketches*, 124.

34. Edersheim, *Sketches*, 109–110.

35. Edersheim, *Sketches*, 228.

36. Edersheim, *Sketches*, 94.

37. Edersheim, *Sketches*, 146–47.

38. Edersheim, *Sketches*, 202.

39. See Matthew 18:5.

40. See Matthew 9:20; 14:36; 23:5; Mark 6:56; Luke 8:44.

41. Edersheim, *Jesus the Messiah*, 431 (1:625).

42. Edersheim, *Jesus the Messiah*, 431–32 (1:625–26).

43. Edersheim, *Jesus the Messiah*, 426, note 12 (1:621).

44. Edersheim, *Jesus the Messiah*, 426 (1:620).

45. Edersheim, *Jesus the Messiah*, 426 (1:621).

46. Edersheim, *Jesus the Messiah*, 436 (1:634).

## CHAPTER SEVEN

# THE JEWISH COMMUNITY

"So LONG AS ISRAEL inhabited Palestine," says the Babylonian Talmud, "the country was wide; but now it has become narrow."[1] There is much historical truth underlying this statement. Each successive change in the country of Palestine left the boundaries of the Holy Land narrower. As yet, it has never actually reached the size Abraham was originally promised (Genesis 15:18), nor the size again promised to the children of Israel during Moses' time (Exodus 23:31). The closest it ever approached to this promised size was during the reign of King David, "when the power of Judah extended as far as the river Euphrates."[2]

"SO LONG AS ISRAEL inhabited Palestine, the country was wide; but now it has become narrow."—The Babylonian Talmud

When our Savior lived in Palestine, the country had already gone through many changes. The Mosaic division of tribes and tribal kingdoms had, after the death of Solomon, given way to the two kingdoms of Judah and Israel. Israel was lost to the Assyrians in the eighth century BC, and Judah to the Babylonians in the sixth century BC. A small number of the Jewish exiles in Babylon had returned to Palestine with Ezra and Nehemiah, and the "Jewish inhabitants of the country consisted either of those who had originally been left in the land, or of the tribes of Judah and Benjamin."[3] Then came Greek conquests and the Macabean rebellion. By the time of Christ's birth, Palestine was governed by Herod the Great. It was a nominally independent kingdom, but it was under the control of Rome. Upon the death of Herod, near the opening of the gospel story, a new but temporary division of Palestine took place among Herod's sons and Rome.

## THE DIVISIONS IN PALESTINE—GALILEE, SAMARIA, JUDEA, AND PERAEA

Edersheim labeled the political divisions of Palestine simply into the four areas of Galilee, Samaria, Judea, and Peraea. Galilee and Peraea were the territories given to Herod Antipas, though he spent most of his time in his palaces in Peraea.[4] This is the same King Herod who would later behead John the Baptist. The Savior did spend some time ministering in Peraea. King Herod became worried, having heard that Jesus may be John raised from the dead, because of his miracles and healings. Herod asked, "Who is this, of whom I hear such things?" (Luke 9:9). He wanted to see Jesus for himself. The Savior was warned about King Herod's interest in him and left Peraea with his Apostles.

### SAMARIA WAS CONSIDERED
a strip of foreign country in Palestine.

The Jews did not regard Samaria as belonging to the Holy Land but saw it as a strip of foreign country, "as the Talmud designates it

(*Chag.* 25*a*), 'a Cuthite strip' or 'tongue' intervening between Galilee and Judea."[5] The Samaritans were ranked with Gentiles and strangers (Matthew 10:5; John 4:9, 20), and "the very term Samaritan was one of reproach" (John 8:48).[6]

The city of Jerusalem and Judea as a whole were the centers of Jewish learning. Religious leaders in Judea sometimes felt contempt and a "supercilious hauteur"[7] for their Jewish brothers up north, especially those living in the Galilean region. In order to distinguish between the material wealth of Galilee versus the supremacy of traditions and academic knowledge of Judea, there was a saying: "If any one wishes to be rich, let him go north; if he wants to be wise, let him come south."[8] These country cousins from Galilee were looked down upon with offensive contempt as shown by Nathanael's slighting question: "Can there any good thing come out of Nazareth?" (John 1:46). The Pharisees rebuked Nicodemus for standing up for Jesus, saying, "Search, and look: for out of Galilee ariseth no prophet." They even mocked him with the question "Art thou also of Galilee?" (John 7:52).

## SANHEDRIN AND RABBIS

The rule of the Romans was chiefly military and fiscal. They collected taxes and made sure the Jews were politically subservient to them. The Sanhedrin was the Jewish ruling body. The name *Sanhedrin* is Greek, but Edersheim speculated that the rabbis may have tried to paraphrase it from Hebrew as " 'sin' (Sinai) 'haderin,' those who repeat or explain the law."[9] Every town had its Sanhedrin, which consisted of 23 members if the town had over 120 men. If the population was smaller, there were only three men on this ruling board.

## THE SANHEDRIN WAS
the Jewish ruling body.

These smaller Sanhedrins are mentioned in the New Testament.[10] These are the councils that Christ warned his disciples would deal roughly with them: "But beware of men: for they will deliver you up to the councils, and they will scourge you in their synagogues" (Matthew 10:17). These Sanhedrin councils took care of all the religious questions and administered judgments in the towns and villages outside of Jerusalem. Sanhedrists were appointed directly from the "supreme authority or Great Sanhedrin, 'the council,' at Jerusalem, which consisted of 71 members."[11] This much larger group or council was the ruling body for the Jews at large. They made decisions about ecclesiastical matters, civil disputes, and political policies.

The members of the Sanhedrin, or Sanhedrists, were supposed to be looked on by the people of their city or village as "learned in the law and of good repute."[12] The special qualifications for the office of Sanhedrist were that the man must be "wise, modest, God-fearing, truthful, not greedy of filthy lucre, given to hospitality, kindly, not a gambler, nor a usurer, nor one who traded in the produce of Sabbatical years, nor yet one who indulged in unlawful games."[13] The members of the Sanhedrin were called elders (Luke 7:3); rulers (Mark 5:22); and "feeders, overseers, shepherds of the flock" (Acts 20:28; 1 Peter 5:2). They were "set apart by 'the laying on of hands,' " by at least three other men who had themselves received ordination. The Sanhedrin body was under a supreme ruler or "head of the synagogue" who would sometimes even exercise sole authority for the council.[14]

The members of the Sanhedrin had the formal title of rabbi bestowed upon them, and they were declared qualified to administer the law. [15] Not all rabbis were members of a Sanhedrin, but all rabbis had to be authorized to teach the law. The office of rabbi had to be set apart by others who held the title of rabbi. A mere storyteller, a preacher, or teller of legends did not need such authorizations. Initially, the first practice was for every rabbi to accredit his own disciples. Later, this right was transferred to the Sanhedrin. This system did cause some abuses.

In the presence of the rabbi and two other assessors, the candidate "had to deliver a Discourse; hymns and poems given him to teach and to act as Judge (to bind and loose, to declare guilty or free). Nay, there seem to have been even orders, according to the authority bestowed on the person ordained."[16] Only after passing these rigorous tests was the candidate then given authority to teach the law.

Rabbis also worked at a trade to make their living. They were not to seek wealth or money from their teaching and judging of the law.

With few exceptions, all the leading rabbinical authorities worked, until it became quite an affectation to engage in hard bodily labor. The Talmud taught, "Whoever does not teach his son a trade is as if he brought him up to be a robber."[17]

The Sanhedrin called into question the authority of Jesus to be a rabbi. They asked him, "By what authority doest thou these things? And who gave thee this authority to do these things?" (Mark 11:28). They were asking Jesus who had ordained him to be a rabbi and given him his authority to be a judge in Israel. His answer was to ask them a question: "I will also ask of you one question, and answer me, and I will tell you by what authority I do these things. The baptism of John, was it from heaven, or of men? Answer me" (Mark 11:29–30). His appeal to John the Baptist was also an appeal to his authority, as Edersheim explained, because John "had borne full witness of the Mission of Christ from the Father and all men counted John, that he was a prophet indeed. . . . They would not, or could not answer! If they said the Baptist was a prophet, this implied not only the authorization of the Mission of Jesus, but the call to believe on Him. On the other hand, they were afraid publicly to disown John."[18] Instead, they answered Jesus with the cowardly answer that they could not tell him. So the Savior answered them, "Neither do I tell you by what authority I do these things" (Mark 11:33).

## PHARISEES AND SADDUCEES

The two great parties of Pharisees and Sadducees are not as much religious sects as "mental directions" in their perceptions and beliefs in connection with questions of eternity. The Pharisees believed in living the traditions of the Jewish religion "to its every tittle and iota."[19] The object of the Pharisees was to observe in the strictest manner, according to the traditional law, or halacha, all the ordinances concerning Levitical purity and religious dues and offerings. Edersheim described a taunt that Sadducees would use against the Pharisees: "The Pharisees would by and by subject the globe of the sun itself to their purifications."[20]

Saduceeism was a "general reaction against the extremes of Pharisaism, springing from moderate and rationalistic tendencies . . . seeking to defend its principles by a strict literalism of interpretation and application."[21] The Sadducees tended to seek their members from the highest ranking families. Because of this, they were very active in political and civil policy and events. For example, the high priestly families belonged to the Sadducee party (Acts 5:17). This is also the reason for the Sadducees to be connected with the temple and especially the temple booths where they acquired so much of their wealth.

There were dogmatic differences between these two religious parties, as well:

1. *The rule of faith and practice.* The Sadducees realized the importance of the Law, or the first five books of Moses, as being their rule of faith and practice, opposing the oral traditionalism of the Pharisees. The Pharisees relied on the oral history and interpretations of the Law as having equal importance to their rules of faith and practice.

2. *After death.* The Sadducees denied the resurrection of the dead. Edersheim quotes Josephus as imputing to them the denial of even the "reward of punishment after death" (War 2.8.14) and the soul perishing with the body (Antiq. 18.1.4). The Pharisees believed in a resurrection of the body and a reuniting of the spirit and a judgment.

3. *The existence of angels and spirits.* Along with their rationalism, Sadducees did not believe in angels and spirits, while the Pharisees did.

4. *Free will and predestination.* The Sadducees accentuated man's free will, while the Pharisees believed in God's foreordination of man. The Pharisees did admit a "partial influence of the human element on what happened, or the co-operation of the human with the Divine."[22]

Despite these differences, Edersheim tried to stress the fact that it is important not to make sweeping categorical statements about the Sadducees or the Pharisees for such simplifications are "grossly unjust."[23] There were Sadducees who lived traditional laws and Pharisees who were involved in civil and political events.

## ESSENES AND NATIONALISTS

Just as the Pharisees and Sadducees were two parties of religious thought with opposing differences, the Essenes and Nationalists expressed contradictory views on civil law and political domination. The Essenes were strict practicing Jews who were similar to the other Jews in Palestine in doctrine, worship, and practice but who were separatists living outside the Jewish body ecclesiastically and physically. They did not look for the kingdom of God as a physical place, but sought the kingdom through spiritual enlightenment away from Jewish society. There were only about four thousand men at a time who were content to live this rigid and spiritually rigorous life.

The Essenes were seeking "absolute purity in separation from the 'material,' which in itself was defiling."[24] Avoiding large cities or towns, their main settlements or colonies were along the shore of the Dead Sea. Their denial of the resurrection of the body comes from their repudiation of the physical, where "a state of perfectness could not have consisted in the restoration of that which, being material, was in itself impure."[25] Their food was prepared with the utmost strictness, and ritual washings were used to clean the body from its impurities. This was an order that required a life of austere purity, devotion, and obedience. In their belief system, there was "no place for either an Aaronic priesthood or bloody sacrifices."[26] They repudiated both, but they did send thank offerings to the temple.

The Essenes were to guard the sacred books belonging to their sect, even at the peril of their life. These books contained sacred scriptures and teachings specific to the order of the Essenes. In 1947, a young goat herder was fortunate to find some of these hidden books of the Essenes—they are now known as the Dead Sea Scrolls.

Many have speculated that John the Baptist was an Essene and that Jesus Christ's teachings were in some way influenced by the Essenes. Edersheim felt strongly that John's doctrine and baptism did not come from this monastic group of Jews: "But of one thing we may feel certain: neither John the Baptist, and his baptism, nor the teaching of Christianity, had any connection with Essenism."[27] Edersheim continued to assert that Christ's teachings definitely did not come from Essenism, since many of Christ's doctrines were even anti-Essenic.[28] Their traditional and strict views on purification and Sabbath day observance more closely resembled the teachings of the Pharisees, rather than the Savior, and they denied a physical resurrection, similar to the belief of the Sadducees. These views were in direct opposition to the teachings of Jesus Christ.

The Nationalist party, or Zealots as they were often called, was made up of Jews who saw the kingdom of God as their political right since they were the children of Israel. They wanted to be rid of heathen rulers and their political control in order to rule their own country, which they felt was their sacred right. The Nationalist party had a marked rise at the time of King Herod the Great, who reigned at Jesus' birth. Guerilla bands traversed Galilee under the leadership of Ezekias and his son Judas. Herod tried mercilessly to suppress these feelings of nationalism with the executions and slaughtering of families. Eleazar, another member of the Galilean Zealots and a grandson of the Ezekias, was the leader of "Israel's forlorn hope and nobly died at Masada, in the closing drama of the Jewish war of independence"[29] in AD 73. This intense nationalist tendency would also play a part in Jesus' history. Even one of his Apostles was a well-known member of this party (Luke 6:15).

Both the Essenes and the Nationalists were seeking the kingdom of God in different ways and in different places; both of them were missing the mark. As Edersheim pointed out, "only the Kingdom of which Jesus was the King was, as He Himself said, not of this world, and of far different conception from that for which the Nationalists [and the Essenes] longed."[30]

## PUBLICANS

The Roman government extracted high taxes from all the countries they conquered. The collection of taxes became a source of revenue, not only for the Roman government but also for those who oversaw the collection of the moneys. Romans would form joint-stock companies "which bought at public auction the revenues of a province at a fixed price, generally for five years. The board had its chairman, or magister, and its offices at Rome. These were the real Publicani or publicans who often underlet certain of the taxes."[31] The Roman Publicani would then employ people who lived in the country—often from the lower classes, sometimes even slaves—as the tax-gatherers. These are the publicans of the New Testament.

The learned Jerusalem scholars looked down on their intellectual and religious inferiors. In particular, the publicans or tax-gatherers of the officers of Rome were condemned by the rabbis. They were "incapable of bearing testimony in a Jewish court of law, of forbidding to receive their charitable gifts, or even to change money out of their treasury, of ranking them not only with harlots and heathens, but with highwaymen and murderers and of even declaring them excommunicate."[32]

Understanding this about the publicans gives us greater understanding of how the Pharisees must have felt when they heard this story taught by Jesus: "Two men went up into the temple to pray; the one a Pharisee, and the other a publican. The Pharisee stood and prayed thus with himself, God, I thank thee, that I am not as other men are, extortioners, unjust, adulterers, or even as this publican. I fast twice in the week, I give tithes of all that I possess. And the publican, standing afar off, would not lift up so much as his eyes unto heaven, but smote upon his breast, saying, God be merciful to me a sinner" (Luke 18:10–13). Humble men, like this despised yet penitent publican, were the kind of men Jesus picked as his Apostles. They were his closest followers, "for every one that exalteth himself shall be abased; and he that humbleth himself shall be exalted" (Luke 18:14).

## HOSPITALITY TO STRANGERS

In the Torah, or the Law, Jehovah taught the Israelites to be hospitable to strangers and give loving care to the poor and sick. The Jewish rabbis at the time of Christ took these teachings very seriously. It was believed that the "entertainment of travelers was as great a matter as the reception of the Shechinah."[33] *Shechinah* was the word used to describe the glory of the Lord physically represented by a cloud of brightness that indicated his presence with the children of Israel[34] (Exodus 3:1–6; 24:16; 1 Kings 8:10). This gives greater meaning to Paul's admonition addressed to the Hebrews: "Be not forgetful to entertain strangers: for thereby some have entertained angels unawares" (Hebrews 13:2). One of the oldest rabbinical commentaries states that whenever "a poor man stands at thy door, the Holy One, blessed be His Name, stands at his right hand. If thou givest him alms, know that thou shalt receive a reward from Him who standeth at his right hand."[35] By helping the poor and those in need, the Jews were receiving the Shechinah, or the glory of the Lord, in their own lives.

Jewish leaders believed that as they helped others in this life, they would be helping themselves achieve a greater reward in the life to come. The rabbis were bidden to imitate God in four respects:

1. He clothed the naked—"Unto Adam also and to his wife did the Lord God make coats of skins, and clothed them" (Genesis 3:21).
2. He visited the sick—"And the Lord appeared unto him in the plains of Mamre: and he sat in the tent door in the heat of the day" (Genesis 18:1).
3. He comforted the mourners—"And it came to pass after the death of Abraham, that God blessed his son Isaac; and Isaac dwelt by the well Lahai-roi" (Genesis 25:11).
4. He buried the dead—"And he buried him in a valley in the land of Moab, over against Bethpeor: but no man knoweth of his sepulcher unto this day" (Deuteronomy 34:6).

The law of the Old Testament taught the rabbis to serve and care for others rather than focus on self. It was similar to James's definition of "pure religion" as becoming undefiled before God by visiting "the fatherless and widows in their affliction and [keeping] himself unspotted from the world" (James 1:27). The rabbis during the time of Christ would have agreed with this definition of religion.

## THE PARABLE OF THE GOOD SAMARITAN

The Savior's teachings took this Old Testament standard of behavior to a higher level. An example of this was the parable of the good Samaritan. The Samaritans and the Jews had no dealings with each other. The Samaritan woman at the well makes the point, "How is it that thou, being a Jew, asketh drink of me, which am a woman of Samaria? For the Jews have no dealings with the Samaritans" (John 4:9). Rabbinical writings declared that "to partake of their bread was like eating swine's flesh,"[36] and additional sayings included: " 'May I never set eyes on a Samaritan' or else, 'May I never be thrown into company with him!' "[37] The Samaritans were the only people the Jews did not have to help. They were unclean.

In order to answer the lawyer's question, "Who is my neighbor?" (Luke 10:29), the Savior targets the rabbinical beliefs of who he is supposed to help. The Jews' separation from others, even a Samaritan, is healed through service and love. In the parable a priest and a rabbi do not stop to help a wounded Jewish man (whom they should help under Jewish law), but a Samaritan cares for his wounds. When the Savior asks the lawyer, "Which now of these three, thinkest thou, was neighbor unto him that fell among the thieves?" (Luke 10:36), the lawyer must acknowledge that it is the Samaritan who is the neighbor, yet he cannot even utter the dreaded word in reply: "Though unwilling to take the hated name of Samaritan on his lips . . . the lawyer was obliged to reply, 'He that showed mercy on him.' "[38]

The Savior was not just teaching the lawyer a lesson; his message extended to all mankind in all periods of time. He was binding us all together as neighbors and ending any separation that may exist between us. Edersheim explained:

> The Parable implies not a mere enlargement of the Jewish ideas, but a complete change of them. It is truly a Gospel-Parable, for the whole old relationship of mere duty is changed into one of love. Thus, matters are placed on an entirely different basis from that of Judaism. The question now is not "Who is my neighbour?"; but "Whose neighbor am I?" The Gospel answers the question of duty by pointing us to love. . . . Become a neighbor to all by the utmost service thou canst do them in their need. And so the Gospel would not only abolish man's enmity, but bridge over man's separation.[39]

## JOHN THE BAPTIST— PREPARING THE WAY

In direct opposition to the rabbinical pride of Jewish leaders at the time of Christ, Edersheim discussed the humility and meekness of John the Baptist. Edersheim had a particular love for John the Baptist. Similar to Edersheim's own feelings of mission, John the Baptist's mission was to prepare the Jews for Christ, setting up the groundwork for their understanding of Jesus' teachings and their acceptance of Jesus as the Messiah. John would have come in contact with the Jewish opinion of the Pharisees, Sadducees, Essenes, and Nationalists. These different trains of thought did not change John the Baptist's message for the Jewish people. None of these people could deter him from his singular mission:

> And now, of a sudden, "the Voice" was heard in the wilderness! It was not that of Pharisee, Sadducee, Essene, or Nationalist—and yet the Baptist combined the best elements of all these directions. He insisted on righteousness, though not in the sense of the Pharisees; nay, his teaching was a protest against their externalism, since it set

aside the ordinances of Traditionalism, though not after the manner of the Sadducees. John also practices asceticism and withdrew from the world, though not in the spirit of the Essenes; and as regarded Nationalism, none so zealous as the Baptist for the Kingship of Jehovah and the rule of heaven, though not as the Nationalists understood it. The Baptist was an altogether unique personality in that corrupt age. Even Herod Antipas heard him; even a Josephus recorded his life and work; even the Pharisees and priests from Jerusalem sent a deputation to inquire—nay, to ask him (so truthful was he, and little suspected of mere fanaticism)—whether he was "the coming One," or Elijah, or one of the prophets.[40]

## "THE BAPTISM OF JOHN,
### was it from heaven, or of men?"

After John baptized the Savior, he continued to baptize in the Jordan River by the village of Salim until he was later cast into prison by King Herod and finally beheaded. While in prison, John's disciples came to him worried about the popularity of Jesus. It seemed to them that everyone was now going to Jesus to be baptized and not to John the Baptist. They commented to John, "Rabbi, he that was with thee beyond Jordan, to whom thou barest witness, behold, the same baptizeth, and all men come to him" (John 3:26). John's disciples were concerned about this change of allegiance. John reminded them, "Ye yourselves bear me witness, that I said, I am not the Christ, but that I am sent before him . . . this my joy therefore is fulfilled. He must increase, but I must decrease"[41] (John 3:28–30).

It did not matter to him that his followers were diminishing. John's joy was full because the Savior's mission was being fulfilled. Edersheim commented on this passage:

> Not to murmur, but even to rejoice in his seeming failure of success, so that his preparatory work merged in the great mission of Christ; and—not in the hour of exaltation, when most of us feel as if we could find room for nobler sentiments, but in the hour of failure,

when we, mostly all, become intensely self-conscious in our disappointments—to express it, not in resignation of humility, but with the calm of joyous conviction of its rightness and meekness. . . . And to me, at least, the moral sublimity of this testimony of John seems among the strongest evidences in confirmation of the Divine claims and the Mission of Christ.[42]

Often life can be depressing and difficult. We can feel underappreciated—like no one cares about us or our feelings. Through the scriptures, we can gain a proper perspective of life's problems. Similar to John the Baptist, it is our testimony of the mission of Christ that will keep us going through sickness, trial, and emotional stress.

Throughout Christ's ministry, the Savior had to deal with the pride of the Jewish religious leaders, especially those living in Jerusalem. Because of their hard hearts, it was the despised Galileans, unlettered fishermen, and excommunicated publicans who became Jesus' closest followers and Apostles. The prideful behavior of the Jerusalem elite was in direct opposition to what Jesus as Jehovah taught in the Old Testament and what Christ taught in the New Testament. The "voice of one crying in the wilderness" (Matthew 3:3) preparing the people for the Messiah's coming was a humble priest, John the Baptist, who wore "raiment of camel's hair and a leathern girdle about his loins" (Matthew 3:4). "What a contrast [were Christ, John the Baptism, and his Apostles] to the Pharisaical notions of the Messiah and His kingdom!"[43]

## NOTES

1. Edersheim, *Sketches*, 7.
2. Edersheim, *Sketches*, 7. See 2 Samuel 8:3–14.
3. Edersheim, *Sketches*, 8.
4. Edersheim, *Jesus the Messiah*, 683 (2:302). See also Bible Dictionary, "Herod," 700–701.
5. Edersheim, *Sketches*, 13.
6. Edersheim, *Sketches*, 13.
7. Edersheim, *Sketches*, 30.
8. Edersheim, *Sketches*, 30,
9. Edersheim, *Sketches*, 89.
10. See Matthew 5:22, 23; 10:17; Mark 13:9.
11. Edersheim, *Sketches*, 89.
12. Edersheim, *Sketches*, 256.

13. Edersheim, *Sketches*, 257. This description comes from the Talmud (*Sanh.* iii, 3). It is very similar Paul's counsel to Timothy in 1 Timothy 3:1–10.
14. See Matthew 9:18; Mark 5:35–36, 38; Luke 8:41; 13:14; Acts 18:8, 17.
15. This is from the Talmud (*Sanh.* 13. b).
16. Edersheim, *Jesus the Messiah*, 737 (2:382).
17. Edersheim, *Sketches*, 174.
18. Edersheim, *Jesus the Messiah*, 738 (2:383).
19. Edersheim, *Jesus the Messiah*, 68 (1:98).
20. Edersheim, *Jesus the Messiah*, 217 (1:313).
21. Edersheim, *Jesus the Messiah*, 217 (1:313).
22. Edersheim, *Jesus the Messiah*, 220 (1:318). For a complete understanding of these four different principles, read pages 218–21 (1:314–20).
23. Edersheim, *Jesus the Messiah*, 217 (1:313).
24. Edersheim, *Jesus the Messiah*, 227 (1:328).
25. Edersheim, *Jesus the Messiah*, 228 (1:329).
26. Edersheim, *Jesus the Messiah*, 228 (1:330).
27. Edersheim, *Jesus the Messiah*, 225 (1:326). Edersheim goes into an in-depth discussion of the Essenes on pages 223–30 (1:322–32).
28. Edersheim, *Jesus the Messiah*, 225 (1:326).
29. Edersheim, *Jesus the Messiah*, 166 (1:240).
30. Edersheim, *Jesus the Messiah*, 167 (1:241).
31. Edersheim, *Sketches*, 54.
32. Edersheim, *Sketches*, 55–56.
33. Edersheim, *Sketches*, 47.
34. Bible Dictionary, "Shechinah," 773.
35. Edersheim, *Sketches*, 47.
36. Edersheim, *Jesus the Messiah*, 277 (1:401).
37. Edersheim, *Jesus the Messiah*, 277 (1:401).
38. Edersheim, *Jesus the Messiah*, 640 (2:240).
39. Edersheim, *Jesus the Messiah*, 640 (2:240).
40. Edersheim, *Lectures*, 355.
41. John 3:29 states, "He that hath the bride is the bridegroom: but the friend of the bridegroom, which standeth and heareth him, rejoiceth greatly because of the bridegroom's voice: this my joy therefore is fulfilled."
42. Edersheim, *Lectures*, 358.
43. Edersheim, *Sketches*, 56.

# Chapter Eight

# The Temple Is the Center of Worship

During the time of the Savior, the temple in Jerusalem was the center of Jewish religious worship no matter where one lived. The love the Jews had for Jerusalem and their temple is illustrated in this thought: "The world is like unto an eye. The ocean surrounding the world is the white of the eye; its black is the world itself; the pupil is Jerusalem; but the image within the pupil is the sanctuary."[1]

The temple was the place where the Savior went from the time he was a boy of twelve to teach his gospel; it was also the place where rituals and rites continued to be performed that were symbolic of his own life's sacrifice on earth. In order to truly understand our Savior's mission, we must gain a grasp of the temple's feasts and festivals, the sacrifices, the mission of the Levitical priests, and the symbols of the temple: "The Temple and its services form, so to speak, part of the life and work of Jesus Christ; part also of his teaching, and of that of his apostles. What connects itself so closely with Him must be of deepest interest."[2]

"THE WORLD IS LIKE unto an eye. The ocean surrounding the world is the white of the eye; its black is the world itself; the pupil is Jerusalem; but the image within the pupil is the sanctuary."—Alfred Edersheim

## THE SHECHINAH— THE GLORY OF THE LORD

The glory of the temple in Jerusalem during Christ's time was felt to be inferior to the first temple built by Solomon. Herod's reconstruction of the temple far surpassed Solomon's temple in architectural splendor and size. But the real elements that gave the temple its glory were gone. The Holy of Holies was empty without the ark of the covenant, the tables of the law, Aaron's budded rod, and the pot of manna. Nor could the high priest be anointed with holy anointing oil since its composition was unknown; nor the will of God be ascertained through the Urim and Thummim, for it was gone. Most important, the Shechinah was not there. The visible presence of the glory of the Lord was gone from the temple.[3]

In Solomon's temple, the Shechinah could be visibly seen by all of the children of Israel: "And it came to pass, when the priests were come out of the holy place, that the cloud filled the house of the Lord, so that the priests could not stand to minister because of the cloud: for the glory of the Lord had filled the house of the Lord" (1 Kings 8:10–11).

The glory of the Lord did return in the presence of the Lord himself during his lifetime visits to the temple. The Savior's presence in the temple during the feasts and festivals would have brought additional light to the dark world the Jews were experiencing under Roman rule. The glory of the Lord's presence was once more in the temple. During the Feast of Tabernacles, huge menorahs were placed in the outside court to illuminate all around the temple. This illumination was intended to be symbolic: "The light shining out of the Temple . . . must have been intended as a symbol . . . of the Shechinah which once filled the Temple."[4] The Savior was now in his holy temple, but after his crucifixion and resurrection, his glory left once more. As Edersheim exclaimed, "Now, the Shechinah has withdrawn to its own place!"[5]

In the spring of 1820, the Shechinah returned to the earth once more.[6] A young boy, Joseph Smith, went into the woods to pray, and he saw, as he describes in is own words, "a pillar of light exactly over my head, above the brightness of the sun, which descended gradually until it fell upon me. . . . When the light rested upon me I saw two Personages, whose brightness and glory defy all description, standing above me in the air. One of them spake unto me, calling me by name and said, pointing to the other—This is My Beloved Son. Hear Him!" (JS—H 1:16–17).

## IN THE SPRING OF 1820,
the Shechinah returned to the earth
once more.

Temples now dot the earth. Each one bears the inscription, "The House of the Lord, Holiness to the Lord." The keys of sealing have been restored and those who officiate in the temples have the priesthood power "to turn the hearts of the fathers to the children, and the children to the fathers, lest the whole earth be smitten with a curse" (D&C 110:15). In the dedication of the temple at Kirtland, Ohio, the first temple in these latter days, the Prophet Joseph Smith dedicated it as "a house to thy name, that the Son of Man might have a place to manifest himself to his people" (D&C 109:5). The glory of his presence has returned to earth once more.

## WITHIN THE HOLY PLACE

The temple complex in New Testament times was organized into various courts and areas of worship. Each one served a certain religious function. The holiness of the temple area restricted those who could enter therein. The outer temple porches and the Court of the Gentiles was where all people could congregate—Jew and Gentile. This formed the outer enclosure of the temple. In the halls or porches around the Court of the Gentiles was a place for friendly meetings and religious discussions. It is in the Court of the Gentiles that the animal booths were kept for people to buy sacrificial animals and where the Savior cleansed the temple twice.

There were eight gates surrounding the temple with the so-called Beautiful Gate being the eastern gate and the principal entrance to the temple. It separated the Court of the Gentiles and the Women's Court. It was here that Peter and John entered the temple after the Savior's resurrection and healed a lame man. Because this man had the coveted begging place near the Beautiful Gate, the Jews knew him and recognized him: "And all the people saw him walking and praising God: and they knew that it was he which sat for alms at the Beautiful gate of the temple: and they were filled with wonder and amazement at that which had happened unto him" (Acts 3:9–10).

The Court of Women was a place of worship for all Jews. This area was restricted from Gentiles entering. There were several large inscriptions warning Gentiles against entry into the temple. Jewish women could worship in this part of the temple, but go no further. All along the court were thirteen chests, or trumpets, for charitable contributions to be placed. Each trumpet had a specific purpose for certain gifts or offerings. This place in the temple was also designated the treasury. "We can also understand how, from the peculiar and known destination of each of these thirteen 'trumpets,' the Lord could distinguish the contributions of the rich who cast in 'of their abundance' from that of the poor widow who of her 'penury' had given 'all the living' that she had (Mark 12:41; Luke 21:1)."[7]

The Court of Israel and the Court of the Priests could be regarded as one area of the temple since it was divided into two by a low balustrade eighteen inches high. The altar was the most prominent object in the Court of Priests. This immense altar of unhewn stones was described in this way:

> A square of not less than 48 feet, and, inclusive of "the horns" 15 feet high. . . . Close by was the great heap of salt, from which every sacrifice must be salted with salt. . . . The four "horns" of the altar were straight, square, hollow prominences . . . into whose silver funnels the drink-offerings and at the Feast of Tabernacles, the water from the Pool of Siloam, were poured. A red line all round

the middle of the altar marked that *above* it the blood of sacrifices intended to be eaten, *below* it that of sacrifices wholly consumed, was to be sprinkled. The system of drainage into chambers below and canals, all of which could be flushed at will, was perfect; the blood and refuse being swept down into Kedron and towards the royal gardens.[8]

The altar of incense was smaller and was always kept burning to signify the prayers of the congregation. There was also the Molten Sea, a great lave or basin for washing, made of brass and supported by "twelve colossal lions, which was drained every evening and filled every morning . . . where twelve priests could wash at the same time."[9]

The Holy House itself was mounted by a flight of twelve steps. In the Holy Place, there were "to the south, the golden candlestick; to the north, the table of shewbread; and beyond them the altar of incense, near the entrance of the Most Holy."[10] Daily, one priest had the honor and distinction of entering the Holy Place to take care of the incense, candles, and twelve loaves of shewbread.

"A wooden partition separated the Most Holy from the Holy Place; and over the door hung the veil."[11] The Holy of Holies was only entered once a year, on the Day of Atonement by the high priest. The place was now empty except for a large stone on which the high priest sprinkled blood on that day. On the day our Savior died on the cross, the veil of the temple "was 'rent in twain from the top to the bottom' when the way into the holiest of all was opened on Golgotha (Matthew 27:51)."[12] That day, the high priest entered into the Holy of Holies, but the high priest bids us all to enter: "Jesus, when he had cried again with a loud voice, yielded up the ghost. And behold, the veil of the temple was rent in twain from the top to the bottom; and the earth did quake, and the rocks rent; And the graves were opened; and many bodies of the saints which slept arose" (Matthew 27:50–52).

## THE PRIESTS

The priests were those who ministered to the people and took care of the holy things at the temple. The Levites were divided into twenty-four courses, or groups, with half of them living in Jerusalem. The other twelve were scattered over the land. "When a course was on duty, all its members were bound to appear in the Temple. Those who stayed away . . . had to meet in the synagogues of their district to pray and fast each day of their week of service."[13]

Everything associated with the priesthood was symbolic. The fundamental design of Israel was to become "a kingdom of priests, and an holy nation" (Exodus 19:5–6). The realization of this blessing will be at his Second Coming; but, the barrier of sin gets in the way of its fulfillment. There were two foundational principles underlying the Levitical priesthood and the sacrifices they perform for the people— reconciliation and mediation. "Even the Hebrew term for priest (*Cohen*) denotes in its root-meaning 'one who stands up for another, and mediates in his cause.' "[14]

> The object of reconciliation was *holiness*. Israel was to be "a holy nation"—reconciled through the "sprinkling of blood;" brought near to, and kept in fellowship with God by that means. The priesthood, as the representative offerers of that blood and mediators of the people, were also to show forth the "holiness" of Israel. . . . The *bodily qualifications* required in the priesthood, the kind of *defilements* which would temporarily or wholly interrupt their functions, their *mode of ordination*, and even every portion, material, and colour of their *distinctive dress* were all intended to express in a symbolical manner this characteristic of holiness.[15]

Originally the office of the high priest was regarded as a lifelong position received through bloodlines and a calling from the Lord, but during the time of the Savior, the high priest calling had degenerated to becoming a matter of "cabal, crime, or bribery."[16] For this temple period, the high priesthood was received by money, not as an appointment from God. It was a political office, not a spiritual calling.

EVERYTHING ASSOCIATED with the priesthood was symbolic. The fundamental design of Israel was to become "a kingdom of priests, and an holy nation" (Exodus 19:5–6).

It seems that the priests of the temple were the ones behind the Savior's final crucifixion. Some of them were overzealous in their keeping of the law and had become blind, "which blindness came by looking beyond the mark, they must need fall; for God hath taken away his plainness from them" (Jacob 4:14). But Edersheim warned not to blame all those who were priests. The Levites were usually the ones who were trying to keep errant Israel in line and following Jehovah. During a time of general spiritual defection, it was the Levites who gathered around Moses: "Then Moses stood in the gate of the camp, and said, Who is on the Lord's side? let him come unto me. And all the sons of Levi gathered themselves together unto him" (Exodus 32:26). In the early Christian church, there was "a great company of the priests [who] were obedient to the faith" (Acts 6:7). Many of the Levite priests became strong members of the early Christian church.

# SACRIFICE

Sacrifice is a central theme of the Old Testament. The location of the Temple Mount was on Mount Moriah, where Abraham offered Isaac to the Lord. It was on this same mount that David saw the hand of the destroying angel stayed, "probably just above where afterwards from the large altar of burnt-offerings the smoke of countless sacrifices rose day by day."[17] Here, Solomon later built the Temple.

Previously, the tabernacle had been used as the center of worship and the place where the ark resided. The ark was a movable yet solid object that could relocate as the children of Israel traveled. Edersheim makes an interesting point that during their wanderings, most of the formal religious practices were not done as frequently. Sacrificial worship did not become a regular practice until the children of Israel were more established in the land:

> Let it be remembered that the special legislative, religious (and even political) institutions of the Pentateuch bear reference to what was then future, rather than to what was then present—to the settled, rather than the migratory, state of the people. Many—I had almost said, most—of these institutions had no place in the wilderness. This holds true in regard to what constitutes the central and really all-determining institution of the Mosaic religious legislation: sacrificial worship. . . . The only sacrifices mentioned in connection

with the Tabernacle are those brought at its consecration and at that of the priesthood, and the offering of incense. . . . Hence the name, which the Tabernacle bears, is not "Tabernacle of sacrifices," . . . but its common designation is "Tabernacle of Meeting" (Ohel Moed) . . . that is, between God and Israel, the place where God would meet with His people.[18]

Israel had been tainted by Egyptian idolatry and the evil influence of generations who had worshipped other gods. When the children of Israel came to their promised land, the worship of the people around Israel was "licentious nature worship."[19] The children of Israel began looking forward to another law to be written in the hearts (Deuteronomy 30:6). The prophets of Israel set before them the coming of the Messiah and the establishment of God's kingdom upon earth as the great hope of Israel and of the world."[20] The animal sacrifices they were asked to make were tokens or symbols of the last great sacrifice of the Lord. Along with the sacrifice of animals, they were also asked to sacrifice a broken heart and a contrite spirit.

Reflecting upon the significance of animal sacrifices performed in the Jewish Temple, Edersheim suggested these were types or symbols of events to come, not mere ceremonial events devoid of inner meaning: "Thus the Old Testament sacrifices were not only symbols, . . . but they already conveyed to the believing Israelite the blessing that was to flow from the future reality to which they pointed."[21]

Sacrificial substitution is a fundamental principle of the Old Testament implying atonement and redemption through vicarious punishment and subsequent forgiveness. These sacrifices required priests to act as mediators between the supplicant and his sacrifice. Yet the priests themselves would change over time, for they were temporal beings who were constantly being renewed by younger priests taking their place. The Israelites were awaiting the time when "He whose Priesthood was perfect, and who on a perfect altar brought a perfect sacrifice, once for all—a perfect Substitute, and a perfect Mediator."[22]

## FEAST OF TABERNACLES

The feasts and festivals of the temple were also symbolic of the Savior as exemplified by the Feast of Tabernacles. It was the most joyous of all the festive seasons because it immediately followed the yearly harvesting of crops. "The harvest-thanksgiving of the Feast of Tabernacles reminded Israel, on the one hand, of their dwelling in booths in the wilderness, while, on the other hand, it pointed to the final harvest when Israel's mission should be completed, and all nations gathered unto the Lord."[23] The feast began five days after the Day of Atonement, the double-holiday eliciting the utmost reverence and awareness of Israel's unique relationship to their God. The Feast of Tabernacles was marked by its unique sacrifices and seven-day celebration wherein the Israelites were commanded to dwell in temporary "booths" made from living tree boughs.[24]

With each dawn of the week-long feast, Levites blew the trumpets and proclaimed, "Our eyes are towards Jehovah." But as Edersheim wrote, "The two most important ceremonies of the Feast of Tabernacles [were] the pouring out of water and the illumination of the Temple."[25] Daily, a priestly procession made its way to the pool of Siloam, from which they filled a golden pitcher with water and carried it back to the Temple, where it was then poured out upon the great altar.[26] Edersheim closes the gap between the rituals and their fulfillment in Jesus Christ. He explains, "It was on that day, after the priest had returned from Siloam with his golden pitcher, and for the last time poured its contents on the base of the altar; after the 'Hallel' had been sung to the sound of the flute, the people responding and worshipping as the priests three times drew the three-fold blasts from their silver trumpets—just when the interest of the people had been raised to its highest pitch, . . . a voice was raised which resounded through the Temple."[27]

"Jesus stood and cried, saying, If any man thirst, let him come unto me, and drink. He that believeth on me, as the scripture hath said, out of his belly shall flow rivers of living water" (John 7:37–38). Edersheim pointed out that in this simple declaration, the significance of the rite was explained and its fulfillment established. Jesus proclaimed himself as the source of their salvation; he was their Deliverer.

As described earlier, the temple was also lit by large menorahs during this feast time. The light would shine out of the temple into the darkness and light up every court in Jerusalem.[28] Once again, Jesus proclaimed himself as the physical fulfillment of this ceremony: "I am the light of the world: he that followeth me shall not walk in darkness, but shall have the light of life" (John 8:12). Through his presence, the Savior had brought back his light into his temple. If the people would follow him, they would also be able to partake of his light and glory. Isaiah prophesied about the Savior bringing back the Shechinah to the temple: "The people that walked in darkness have seen a great light: they that dwell in the land of the shadow of death, upon them hath the light shined" (Isaiah 9:2).

## NOTES

1. Edersheim, *Temple*, 16.
2. Edersheim, *Temple*, vii.
3. Edersheim, *Temple*, 37.
4. Edersheim, *Temple*, 226.
5. Edersheim, *Temple*, 17.
6. Bible Dictionary, "Shechinah," 773.
7. Edersheim, *Temple*, 25–26.
8. Edersheim, *Temple*, 30–31.
9. Edersheim, *Temple*, 32.
10. Edersheim, *Temple*, 34.
11. Edersheim, *Temple*, 34.
12. Edersheim, *Temple*, 34.
13. Edersheim, *Temple*, 36.
14. Edersheim, *Temple*, 57.
15. Edersheim, *Temple*, 58.
16. Edersheim, *Temple*, 65.
17. Edersheim, *Temple*, 37.
18. Edersheim, *Lectures*, 235–37.
19. Edersheim, *Lectures*, 235.
20. Edersheim, *Lectures*, 225.
21. Edersheim, *Temple*, 75.
22. Edersheim, *Temple*, 76.
23. Edersheim, *Temple*, 213.
24. See Leviticus 23:34.
25. Edersheim, *Temple*, 227.
26. Edersheim, *Temple*, 220–21.
27. Edersheim, *Temple*, 222–23.
28. Edersheim, *Temple*, 226.

# CHAPTER NINE

# PROPHETS AND PROPHECY

RABBIS HAVE ASKED THE question, "Why was Adam, a single human being, created first rather than along with other humans?"[1] In the Talmud, the reason is given that God created Adam as a single life to teach the value of an individual to all future generations: "Anyone who destroys even one life, destroys an entire world. And he who preserves a single human life has saved the equivalent of the entire world."[2] Also, Adam as a single creation reminds all people of the world that they spring from the same parents without ugly comparisons of whose parents were greater or better. This is supposed to bring peace to the world.

The prophets are to bring the good news of the gospel of Jesus Christ to all peoples throughout all dispensations. He is the Prince of Peace. They are to prophesy of him and help establish his kingdom on the earth. From the time of Adam, Christ has taught that "all things have their likeness, and all things are created and made to bear record of me" (Moses 6:63). It is of great importance for us to know that God " 'created all things by Jesus Christ' (Ephesians 3:9); and further, that 'all things were created by Him, and for Him' (Colossians 1:16), and that 'of Him, and through Him, and to Him are all things (Romans 11:36).' This gives not only unity to all creation, but places it in living connection with our Lord Jesus Christ."[3] As we individually follow the prophets and their words, we will find peace in our lives, which will eventually bring peace to the world and establish his kingdom here on earth—"for he is our peace" (Ephesians 2:14).

## THE ROLE OF PROPHETS AND PROPHECY

Prophets do not simply prophesy or foretell future events; they also reprove, reform, and instruct. Edersheim describes it beautifully: "The prophet sees the future in the light of the present, and the present in the light of the future: he wells forth of the waters of God, and he is the man of God."[4] The Lord sent prophets to be his messengers, giving relevant instructions from God to all people. Sometimes, those relevant instructions will include forewarning of future events and things they must do to prepare if they want to survive spiritually and physically. Often, humanity does not listen to the prophets God sends. They do not want to hear the words of warning that could save them.

The story of Noah is a simple example of the faith of prophets to be obedient to God and the long-suffering nature of God toward his children. The tender loving kindness of Jehovah appears in the scriptures: "It repented the Lord that he had made man on the earth, and it grieved him" (Genesis 6:6). Edersheim translated the word *grieved* as meaning literally "it pained into His heart."[5] Even though there seemed to be universal corruption, "Noah found grace in the eyes of the Lord" (Genesis 6:8). In stark contrast to others around him, Noah "was a just man and perfect in his generations, and Noah walked with God" (Genesis 6:9).

"IN SHORT PROPHECY cannot be compressed within the four corners of fact: it is not merely tidings about the future. It is not dead, but instinct with undying life, and that life is divine."—Alfred Edersheim

For the next 120 years, Noah built the ark under the direct super-vision of Jehovah.[6] During this time, Noah acted as a preacher of righ-teousness: "Noah preached righteousness, warning of the judgment to come, and still exhibiting his faith in his practice by continuing to provide an ark of refuge."[7] Noah wanted to save his people physically and spiritually. Jehovah wanted to give his children another chance to repent and change. Noah lived a life of faith, preaching in faith and working in faith on the ark: "By faith Noah, being warned of God of things not seen as yet, moved with fear, prepared an ark to the saving of his house; by which he condemned the world, and became heir of the righteousness which is by faith" (Hebrews 11:7). Noah forewarned the people about the flood and built an ark for them to enter. But only part of his family listened. All the rest, including some of his kinfolk, perished in the flood.

Noah prophesied the coming of the flood and the prophecy was fulfilled. There is a moral aspect to prophecy that goes past its mere ful-fillment in time. It teaches future generations the importance of acting on faith, trusting in God, and obeying God's commandments: "In short, prophecy cannot be compressed within the four corners of a fact: it is not merely tidings about the future. It is not dead, but instinct with undying life, and that life is divine. There is a moral aspect in prophecy to all generations. Under one aspect of it, it prepares for the future, and this is the predictive element of it. Under its other aspect it teaches les-sons of the present to each generation; and is its moral aspect."[8]

Following generations could learn from the judgment of the flood. The destruction of the flood came upon the ungodly; while the people of God, who chose to follow his prophet, were preserved. This would be the pattern for all time.

## PREPARING A COVENANT PEOPLE

Modern prophets have taught us that before we came to earth, we enjoyed a loving relationship with our Heavenly Father and Jesus Christ. Through Adam, a covenant relationship with God and our Savior continued on this earth. As we understand the covenant of the Old Testament, we will gain a greater understanding of the eternal relation-ship God has had with his people throughout the history of man's mortal probation. This covenant relationship started premortally, continues through this earth life, and will continue throughout eternity.

The scriptures and the words of living prophets explain the covenant that we are to make. In the story of the Garden of Eden, we are successively shown man's original position and relationship toward God; then his fall, and the consequent need of redemption; and finally, God's gracious provision of mercy through a Redeemer. From Edersheim's view, the history of the covenant and of the covenant-people began with Father Abraham.[9] But we know through restored scriptures and modern prophets, these covenants started with Adam and have been established since the foundation of the world. Through this covenant relationship between God and man, God's richest promises are unfolded, and God's gracious dealings with man are seen.

The covenant and promises given to Abraham express the "ideal object of Israel's calling, and hence of their history and institutions."[10] The first promise was, "In thee shall all the families of the earth be blessed" (Genesis 12:3). This promise is so fundamental that it is repeated three times to Abraham (Genesis 12:3, 18:18; 22:18); it is renewed to Isaac (Genesis 26:4); and it is reiterated to Jacob (Genesis 28:14). Edersheim saw in this promise a divine meaning that would become "the planting-ground for the Kingdom of God, whence in the fulness of time and of preparation it would be transplanted into the heathen world; in other words, the blessings of that kingdom were to be imparted through Israel to the world at large."[11]

Abraham is an example for all men of surrendering your life to God. Edersheim explained, "At God's bidding, Abraham has necessarily given up country, kindred, and home, and then his paternal affection towards Ishmael. It yet remained to give up even Isaac after the flesh, so as to receive him again spiritually."[12] Abraham represents a man who lived a life of faith following the covenants he had made with God.

Abraham was seen as a righteous man by all the nations of the world. At Abraham's death, the Talmud describes all the great ones of the world gathering as mourners and exclaiming, "Woe to the world which has lost its guide; woe to the ship which has lost its helmsman."[13]

While reading the scriptures, the inconvenience and burden of living all the commandments of God may seem overwhelming and difficult. Yet Edersheim felt his Jewish upbringing helped him see the uplifting qualities of commandments: "It is a beautifully significant idea, that the Jews, after fulfilling any commandment or ordinance of the Law, specially thank God for having given it—to show that the Law is not a burden, but a privilege."[14]

The Mishna explains why the Shema (discussed earlier), or the creed of the Jews, is placed in a certain order. In the first scripture (Deuteronomy 6:4–9), the Lord asks his children to hear him and love him with all one's heart, soul, and strength. His children are asked to take upon themselves the yoke of his kingdom or the kingdom of heaven. Then, in Deuteronomy 11:13–15, they are asked to take upon themselves the yoke of his commandments. In the final scripture, his children are asked to follow him always "and remember all the commandments of the Lord and do them" (Numbers 15:39).

This understanding of the Shema brings a singular meaning to the Savior's invitation: "Come unto me, all ye that labor and are heavy laden, and I will give you rest. Take my yoke upon you, and learn of me; for I am meek and lowly in heart; and ye shall find rest unto your souls. For my yoke is easy, and my burden is light" (Matthew 11:28–30). Edersheim further explains, "These words must indeed have had a special significance to those who remembered the Rabbinic lesson as to the relation between the kingdom of heaven and the commandments, and they would now understand how by coming to the Saviour they would first take upon them 'the yoke of the kingdom of heaven' and then that of 'the commandments,' finding this 'yoke easy' and the 'burden light.' "[15]

The commandments will actually make our burdens lighter here on earth; by living them, we are not lifting our burdens alone. The Savior will make our yoke easier by picking up our load of cares.

# ESTABLISHING THE KINGDOM OF GOD

Part of the Abrahamic Covenant was the blessing of land to Abraham and his seed that would be theirs throughout eternity: "And I will give unto thee, and to thy seed after thee, the land wherein thou art a stranger, all the land of Canaan, for an everlasting possession; and I will be their God" (Genesis 17:8). The deepest underlying thought of the Jewish state was "that Palestine was the land of God, and Israel the people of God; that Jehovah and Jehovah alone was King; that His was the sole universal kingdom, against which those outside Israel were in high-handed rebellion. All else—even their excesses—were their inferences from this fundamental position."[16]

Because of these promises, the children of Israel began to see Palestine as the Lord's kingdom and the sole universal kingdom for the world. All other nations represented the enemies of God. They interpreted "so many of the predictions concerning the kingdom of God [as] presented under a particularistic and national aspect . . . Zion, Israel, Moab, or else the then present enemies of the people of God . . . those nations did at that time actually represent the enemies of the kingdom of God."[17] But Edersheim understood the eternal perspective of the object and mission of Israel, which was that "all nations were through their ministry to become really the possession of God: a kingdom of priests, a holy people; for all the earth as well as Israel was God's. And the realization of this would be the kingdom of God on earth."[18]

When Joshua and the children of Israel first entered the promised land, the first necessity of Israel was to fight for existence. They had to obtain possession of their land, achieved only after continual warfare. They were surrounded by hostile nations and independent clans under separate kings. A victory in one locality might be decisive; but then they would advance a few miles and the new territory would have a new king and new people to fight.

After they were able to maintain their land, the laws, the worship, the institutions, and the mission of Israel were intended to express these two things: acknowledgment of God and dependence upon God. Edersheim explained how all parts of Israel's leadership were instituted to help Israel acknowledge God:

> The patriarchs were the Servants of the Lord; Israel was the Servant of the Lord; and their three-fold representative institutions expressed the same idea. The Priest was to be wholly the Servant of the Lord (smallest transgression brought his destruction or removal). The King was not to bear rule in the manner of heathen princes, but to be the Servant of the Lord, in strictest subordination to Jehovah. (Saul, despite his nobler qualities, became an antichrist while David, despite his faults, constantly acknowledged God's kingship and was saved). Third, the Prophet was simply the Servant of the Lord.[19]

Israel was constantly taught by prophets to repent and return to following the Lord, but Israel would not listen. They were easily persuaded to follow other gods. Finally, the kingdom of Israel was divided and destroyed. Edersheim's optimism saw Israel's exile as a way to further the kingdom of God:

> It seems a defective, if not a false, view of it to regard the Babylonish exile as simply a Divine punishment for the sins, especially the idolatry, of Israel. I venture to assert that there is nothing merely negative, or exclusively punitive, in the Divine dealings in history, especially in what bears on the Kingdom of God. Every step taken is also a step in advance, even though, in making it, something had to be put down and crushed. It was not otherwise with the Babylonian exile. Assuredly one aspect of it was punitive of Israel's sin. But that, by which this punishment was effected, also brought Israel a step nearer the goal of its world-mission.[20]

## THE MESSIANIC HOPE

The hope for the Messiah—the Deliverer, the Anointed One who would be King and bring peace to the world—was instilled in the children of the covenant since the time of Adam and continued throughout the Old Testament to the time of Christ. In the Garden of Eden, the Messiah promised: "He shall bruise thy head, and thou shalt bruise his heel" (Moses 4:21). In the great mortal conflict between humanity and evil, "Humanity will be ultimately victorious, in and through its Representative: crush the head of the Serpent, although in this not without damage, hurt, and the poison of death."[21] This promise of victory in the midst of difficulty "ennobles our human nature by representing it as moral; it bears a promise; it contains a prophecy."[22]

After the return of broken Israel, the hope for a Messiah to reunite the children of Israel and reinstitute their kingdom was rekindled. Edersheim commented, "It is true that the Apocrypha preserve silence about the Person of the Messiah. But this, not because the Messianic idea was ignored, but because it was apprehended and presented in another form. It was no longer the Person of the Messiah, but the Messianic times, which engaged the expectancy of the people."[23]

During the Savior's time, the hope for the coming of the Messiah was burning bright. There was a nationalistic hope that the Messiah would overthrow the Roman government and reign supreme over their homeland: "Never did the Messianic hopes of the inspired Prophets rise higher; never was their faith wider in its range, or brighter in its glow; never their utterance of it more passionately assured, than when Israel had sunk to the lowest stage of outward depression. . . . In truth it scarcely seems exaggeration to say, that throughout the history of Israel we can trace the times of bitterest sorrows by their brightest Messianic expectations."[24]

## "ALL PROPHECY POINTS to the Kingdom of God and to the Messiah as its King."—Alfred Edersheim

Because of these expectations, the people were looking for the Messiah to appear. Through the words of the Old Testament prophets, the Jews knew that a Messiah was coming. They were hoping for it to come soon and save them from their physical bondage: "Christianity in its origin appealed to a great Messianic expectancy, the source and spring of which must be sought not in the post-exilian period, but is found in the Old Testament itself. The whole Old Testament is prophetic. Its special predictions form only a part, although an organic part, of the prophetic Scriptures; and all prophecy points to the Kingdom of God and to the Messiah as its King."[25]

Edersheim points out the fact that Israel still did not understand their mission. They had lost sight of what they were really supposed to do; yet, as they became more and more a part of the world, they were also preparing the world for the kingdom to come: "If Israel had been faithful to its mission, it would have widened to embrace the kingdoms of the world. Israel unfaithful to it, was merged in them, subdued by them. Yet even so, it also fulfilled, in its punishment, its mission—in dying gave up its pearl—bringing mankind a step nearer to the truer realization of the kingdom of God in its world-wide bearing."[26]

## MINGLING NATIONALISM WITH THE MESSIANIC HOPE

Just before the Savior's birth, many of the Jewish people mingled their feelings of nationalism with a messianic hope for a Deliverer. The zealots, many of them living in Galilee, were men of action, passion, and hope. As Edersheim so eloquently describes it, "So patriotism and religion—both in abnormal forms—mingled. They whetted their daggers to the sound of psalms, and sharpened their swords to the martial music of prophetic utterances, which to them seemed only denunciations and imprecations on the enemy."[27]

These nationalistic hopes for a political Deliverer changed the Jewish vision of the Messiah. Their vision was a Messiah-Warrior-King who would come with swords in hand to wipe out their enemies: "The Messiah was no longer a Prince of peace and the Reconciler of the world. The Messianic times were still those of 'the kingdom'—but of one of conquest, of the reinstatement and triumph of Israel, and of the subjection of the Gentile world."[28]

This messianic hope was the central idea of the Jewish religion and Jewish nation. Because of the political supremacy of heathen nations felt by the Jews for generations, it is not surprising that they were asking in their hearts: "Messiah, when will you come?" Edersheim commented, "And such was the spell of the Messianic idea, such the hold it had upon the genius and life of the Jewish nation, that—as we have seen—even so unscrupulously selfish a writer as Josephus could not suppress all reference to it—and this, in works intended for his Roman masters. . . . And how could it be otherwise? The Jew must cease to be a Jew—in any other than the negative sense of opposition to other creeds—if he gives up the messianic hope which is the central idea of his religion."[29]

## THE REALITY OF JESUS CHRIST AS THE MESSIAH

The hoped-for Messiah was in sharp contrast to the life and teachings of Jesus Christ. He was born and lived in humble circumstances; he taught civil obedience; he spoke words of love, kindness, and forgiveness. His preaching about the kingdom of God was very different from the Jews' conception: "Blessed are they which are persecuted for righteousness sake: for theirs is the kingdom of heaven" (Matthew 5:10). Edersheim commented:

> Not so did the God-sent Christ understand, nor yet would He so establish the kingdom of His Father in Heaven. Christ was King—but as meek and lowly, and as, symbolically, making His Royal entry into Jerusalem riding on an ass, the foal of an ass. In view of the opposition of a hostile world, He also must found His kingdom in blood—but in His own Blood, which His enemies shed; not in theirs, which He shed. He also must conquer all enemies, and subdue them to His kingdom; yet not by outward means, but by the moral power of the Truth, and by the constraining influence of His Spirit, working inward and willing submission. His kingdom was not of this world; therefore did His followers not fight for it. The true kingdom of God was within: it was righteousness, and peace, and joy in the Holy Ghost.[30]

The Old Testament had not been misleading in its prophecies and teachings. Edersheim observed, "For, properly understood, the Scripture is all full of Christ, and all intended to point to Christ as our only Saviour. It is not only the law, which is a schoolmaster unto Christ, nor the types, which are shadows of Christ, nor yet the prophecies, which are predictions of Christ; but the whole Old Testament history is full of Christ."[31]

For those who heard the Savior's voice and recognized Jesus Christ as their Messiah, their eyes and ears were opened: "They should see with their eyes, and hear with their ears, and should understand with their heart, and should be converted, and I should heal them" (Matthew 13:15). Even though other Jews physically saw and heard Jesus Christ, they did not hear and see their Messiah, "for this people's heart is waxed gross, and their ears are dull of hearing and their eyes they have closed" (Matthew 13:15). Jesus taught that "for judgment I am come into this world, that they which see not might see; and that they which see might be made blind" (John 9:39).

As a Jew himself, Edersheim was able to see the Messiah in Jesus' words and in his life. From his study of Old Testament prophets, he recognized the prophecies fulfilled in the life of the Savior. His testimony was that "Christ is indeed 'the end of the Law for righteousness,' to Whom all the ordinances of the Old Testament had pointed, and in Whom alone, alike the people and the history of Israel find their meaning."[32]

# NOTES

1. Bleefeld and Shook, *Saving the World Entire*, 42 (Talmudic source: *Sanhedrin 37a–b*).
2. Bleefeld and Shook, *Saving the World Entire*, 42.
3. Edersheim, *Bible History*, 12.
4. Edersheim, *Lectures*, 75.
5. Edersheim, *Bible History*, 27.
6. Edersheim, *Bible History*, 28.
7. Edersheim, *Bible History*, 30.
8. Edersheim, *Lectures*, 38.
9. Edersheim, *Bible History*, 9–10.
10. Edersheim, *Bible History*, 44.
11. Edersheim, *Bible History*, 44.
12. Edersheim, *Bible History*, 72.
13. Edersheim, *Bible History*, 44 (Talmudic source: Baba B, p. 91*a*).
14. Edersheim, *Tohu-va-Vohu*, 1.
15. Edersheim, *Sketches*, 247.
16. Edersheim, *Lectures*, 327.
17. Edersheim, *Lectures*, 35.
18. Edersheim, *Lectures*, 45.
19. Edersheim, *Lectures*, 45.
20. Edersheim, *Lectures*, 297.
21. Edersheim, *Lectures*, 33–34.
22. Edersheim, *Lectures*, 34.
23. Edersheim, *Lectures*, 316.
24. Edersheim, *Lectures*, 8.
25. Edersheim, *Lectures*, 24.
26. Edersheim, *Lectures*, 45.
27. Edersheim, *Lectures*, 330.
28. Edersheim, *Lectures*, 317–18.
29. Edersheim, *Lectures*, 320–21.
30. Edersheim, *Lectures*, 327–28.
31. Edersheim, *Bible History*, 8.
32. Edersheim, *Temple*, viii.

# CHAPTER TEN

# THE MIRACLES OF CHRIST'S BIRTH AND LIFE

THERE IS A TALMUDIC story that the great Caesar wanted to confront the God of the Jews. Caesar summoned a rabbi to tell the rabbi his desire to see their God. The rabbi tried to dissuade Caesar from his request. Caesar continued to press the issue, telling the rabbi that he would arrange a large banquet for God and the rabbi was to invite him to come. Caesar planned the event, but just before it was to take place a huge wind swept everything into the sea. Caesar tried again, but torrential winds washed everything away. Finally, Caesar asked the rabbi why this was happening. The rabbi "explained that the wind and the rain were merely the sweepers and sprinklers that precede God. Caesar listened intently, and finally understood he would never observe the presence of God."[1]

In this parable, Caesar's worldly wealth and riches are no match for the power of God. He misunderstands the nature of God and his relationship to him. Jehovah would not come down at his bidding. He would only come when he determined it was time. Caesar was similar to those who, during Jesus' time, needed to see in order to believe. They wanted physical proof of Jesus' divinity. Certain scribes and Pharisees asked him: "Master, we would see a sign from thee" (Matthew 12:38). The Savior answered them: "An evil and adulterous generation seeketh after a sign" (Matthew 12:39).

Yet Christ's life was full of signs and miracles. Through him, "the blind receive their sight, and the lame walk, the lepers are cleansed, and the deaf hear, the dead are raised up, and the poor have the gospel preached to them" (Matthew 11:5). His condescension to be born on earth and his subsequent Atonement for all mankind were his greatest miracles. They truly did manifest his love for each one of us.

All the Old Testament and Book of Mormon prophets looked forward to this day. Nephi saw this great miracle six hundred years before it happened: "And I looked and beheld the virgin again, bearing a child in her arms. And the angel said unto me: Behold the Lamb of God, yea, even the Son of the Eternal Father! Knowest thou the meaning of the tree which thy father saw? And I answered him, saying: Yea, it is the love of God, which sheddeth itself abroad in the hearts of the children of men; wherefore, it is the most desirable above all things" (1 Nephi 11:20–22).

Edersheim had also looked forward to the miracle of the Messiah. He saw the miracles of his life as messages of love and a further testimony of his divinity. He wrote, "Miracles are of chief value as the evidence of a communion between heaven and earth."[2]

## THE MIRACLES OF CHRIST'S BIRTH

Jesus Christ was born in Bethlehem in "utmost earthly humility,"[3] in the shadow of the magnificent palace-fortress of King Herod. Bethlehem was to be the birthplace of the Messiah by prophetic designation (Micah 5:2). Yet this small town was a most unlikely place for the Savior to be born. Edersheim describes the pastures beyond Bethlehem where the flocks of sheep grazed. There was a tower called Migdal Eder, or the "watch-tower of the flock," where priestly shepherds looked for stray sheep that would be sacrificed at the Jerusalem Temple. These sheep were destined for sacrifice, and priestly-shepherds watched over them. The herald angel announced the birth and the attendant angels burst forth in song, proclaiming the "announcement of the Kingdom coming."[4] These shepherds would take the sheep to the temple in Jerusalem, where they would readily tell others about the miracle they had seen on their "night of wonder." The Messiah had come, for they had seen him:

> We know that, on the night in which our Saviour was born, the angels' message came to those who probably alone of all in or

near Bethlehem were "keeping watch." For, close by Bethlehem, on the road to Jerusalem, was a tower, known as Migdal Eder, the "watch-tower of the flock." For here was the station where shepherds watched their flocks was this, that if animals were found as far from Jerusalem as Migdal Eder, and within that circuit on every side, the males were offered as burnt offerings, the females as peace-offerings. . . . It seems of deepest significance, almost like the fulfillment of type, that those shepherds who first heard tidings of the Saviour's birth, who first listened to angels' praises, were watching flocks destined to be offered as sacrifices in the Temple. There was the type and here the reality. At all times Bethlehem was among "the least" in Judah—so small that the Rabbis do not even refer to it in detail. The small village-inn was over-crowded, and the guests from Nazareth found shelter only in the stable, whose manger became the cradle of the King of Israel. It was here that those who tended the sacrificial flocks, heaven-directed, found the Divine Babe—significantly the first to see Him, to believe, and to adore. But this is not all. It is when we remember, that presently these shepherds would be in the Temple, meet those who came thither to worship and to sacrifice, that we perceive the full significance of what otherwise would have seemed scarcely worthwhile noticing in connection with humble shepherds: "And when they had seen it, they made known abroad the saying which was told them concerning this child. And all they that heard it wondered at those things which were told them by the shepherds" (Luke 2:17–18). Moreover, we can understand the wonderful impression made on those in the courts of the Temple, as while they selected their sacrifices, the shepherds told the about the speedy fulfillment of all these types in what they had themselves seen and heard in that night of wonder.[5]

### "IT SEEMS OF DEEPEST
significance, almost like the fulfillment of type, that those shepherds who first heard tidings of the Saviour's birth, who first listened to angel's praises, were watching flocks destined to be offered as sacrifices to the Temple."—Alfred Edersheim

His birth would have another miracle or sign associated with it. A new star was seen in the heavens. There was a Jewish prophecy that foretold of a star coming at the birth of the Messiah. Robert Millet referenced Edersheim's commentary on the appearance of the star:

> There is, however, testimony which seems to us not only reliable, but embodies most ancient Jewish tradition. It is contained in one of the smaller *Midrashim*. . . . The so-called Messiah-Haggadah (*Aggadoth Mashiach*) opens as follows: *"A star shall come out of Jacob.* There is a Boraita in the name of the Rabbis: The heptad in which the Son of David cometh—in the *first* year, there will not be sufficient nourishment; in the *second* year the arrows of famine are launched; in the *third*, a great famine; in the *fourth*, neither famine nor plenty; in the fifth, great abundance and the *Star shall shine forth from the East and this is the Star of the Messiah."*[6]

The Magi, or priest-sages,[7] came to follow the new star. Edersheim does discuss various possibilities of who these men were and where they came from. They could have been part of the Medes and Persians, where a large Jewish Diaspora lived. He also speculates that these men might have come from Arabia, since from "120 bc to the sixth century of our era, the kings of Yemen professed the Jewish faith."[8]

Innocently, they went to King Herod expecting him to know where this long awaited child was. After assembling all the learned rabbis, Herod asked where the Messiah was to be born. He directed the wise men to Bethlehem. After finding the child, they were to return so Herod himself could pay homage to the child.

When they did not return, Herod had all of the male children of the town of Bethlehem slain in fulfillment of prophecy: "In Rama was there a voice heard, lamentation, and weeping, and great mourning, Rachel weeping for her children, and would not be comforted, because they are not" (Matthew 2:17–18; Jeremiah 31:15). The recording of this heinous crime is not found in any historical records during Herod's reign, which may seem strange. Yet Edersheim estimated that the small town of Bethlehem had a population of only one to two thousand and a very high infant mortality rate. He estimated an annual birthrate of about thirty, and the number of baby boys killed probably not being more than twenty.[9]

Herod's reign of blood and terror was full of such brutalities. Edersheim explains, "The slaughter was entirely in accordance with the character and former measure of Herod. Nor do we wonder, that it remained unrecorded by Josephus, since on other occasions also he has omitted events which to us seem important. The murder of a few infants in an insignificant village might appear scarcely worth notice in a reign stained by so much bloodshed."[10] Edersheim is quick to point out, "But the deed was none the less atrocious; and these infants may justly be regarded as the 'protomartyrs,' the first witnesses of Christ."[11]

## THE MIRACLES THAT JESUS PERFORMED

The first recorded miracle of Jesus' ministry was at the marriage feast in Cana of Galilee. He attended this feast as a part of the family. When they ran out of wine, his mother came to him saying, "They have no wine" (John 2:3). Jesus' answer may seem harsh: "Woman, what have I to do with thee?" (John 2:4). Edersheim compares this answer to the answer the young boy Jesus gave his mother when she found him in the temple and he answered her, "Wist ye not that I must be about my Father's business?" (Luke 2:49). "It is a truth which we must ever learn, and yet are ever slow to learn in our questionings and suggestings, alike as concerns His dealings with ourselves and His rule of His Church, that the highest and only true point of view is 'the Father's business,' not our personal relationship to Christ. . . . For, there is ever deepest unity and harmony in the truest Life, the Life of Life."[12]

Mary turned from him and told the servants to do whatever Jesus told them to do. They filled the water-pots to the brim and the water was turned into wine. Edersheim repeats the "coarse proverbial joke"[13] that "the conscious water saw its God, and blushed."[14] Edersheim's own description of the miracle is that Jesus transformed the "water of legal purification into the wine of the new dispensation."[15]

"MIRACLES ARE OF CHIEF VALUE
as the evidence of a communion between
heaven and earth."—Alfred Edersheim

Edersheim mentions how some people try to explain away or figure out how Jesus did his miracles. In Edersheim's mind, "For miracle it is, and will ever remain; not, indeed, magic, nor arbitrary power, but power with a moral purpose, and that the highest. And we believe it, because this thing is the first of all those miracles in which the Miracle of Miracles gave a sign, and manifested forth His glory—the glory of His Person, the glory of His Purpose, and the glory of His Work."[16]

Later in his ministry, the Savior was in Jerusalem at the pool of Bethesda. The popular idea was that "an Angel descended into the water, causing it to bubble up, and that only he who first stepped into the pool would be cured. As thus only one person could obtain benefit, we may imagine the lamentations of the many who would, perhaps, day by day, be disappointed in their hopes."[17] An impotent man lay by the edge of the pool. The Savior asked him, "Wilt thou be made whole?" (John 5:6). The man did not understand and asked for his help to get into the water. Instead, the Savior told him, "Rise, take up thy bed, and walk" (John 5:8). "Forth he stepped into God's free air, a new man. . . . These directions had been bound up with the very word 'Rise' in which his healing had come. That was enough for him. And in this lay the beginning and root of his inward healing. Here was simple trust, unquestioning obedience to the unseen, unknown, but real Saviour. For he believed Him."[18]

The Savior was drawn to people in need. Edersheim explained that this was his reason for coming to this earth—to take upon himself the sins and afflictions of the world—that is the Miracle:

> What would we expect Him to have done? . . . but to do . . . [when] brought into contact with misery, disease, and death without their being removed. That power went forth from him always, every-where, and to all, is absolutely necessary, if He was the Son of God, the Saviour of the world. And so the miracles, as we mistakingly term the result of the contact of God with man, of the Immanuel (God with us), are not only the golden ladder which leads up to The Miracle, God manifest in the flesh, but the steps by which He descends from His height to our lowliness.[19]

There are numerous miracles of the Savior. Edersheim mentions that people often get too involved in the miracles of Christ: "Most people's minds are so coarsely constituted that they dwell exclusively upon miracles: they are either their great evidence for Christianity, or else their great objection to it."[20] The healing power of the Savior is not just through physical miracles, but also spiritual conviction of power to save our souls for "Jesus is the Christ, the Son of God; and that believing ye might have life through His Name" (John 20:31).

"HIS GOING INTO DEATH was His final conflict with Satan for man, and on his behalf. By submitting to it He took away the power of Death; He disarmed Death by burying his shaft in His own Heart."—Alfred Edersheim

## THE MIRACLE OF HIS DEATH

At the end of his life, Christ retired to the Garden of Gethsemane to pray and to take upon himself sin and death. As the Son of God who lived a sinless life, he was not subject to Satan; he was not born with the taste of death in his soul. Yet he submitted vicariously "to the deepest humiliation, and [paid] the utmost penalty: Death—all Death. . . . His going into Death was His final conflict with Satan for man, and on his behalf. By submitting to it He took away the power of Death; He disarmed Death by burying his shaft in His own Heart."[21]

He was by himself in this conflict, as he had been in his wilderness experience with Satan. He would look up to his Father for support, yet he needed to do this on his own:

> Alone as in His first conflict with the Evil One in the Temptation in the wilderness, must the Saviour enter on the last contest. With what agony of soul He took upon Him now and there the sins of the world, and in taking expiated them, we may learn from this account of what passed, when, with strong crying and tears unto Him that was "able to save Him from death," He "offered up prayers and supplications" (Heb. 5:7). And—we anticipate it already—with these results: that He was heard; that He learned obedience by the things which He suffered; that He was made perfect; and that He became:

to us the Author of Eternal Salvation, and before God, a High-Priest after the order of Melchizedek. Alone—and yet even this being "parted from them" (. . . Luke 22:41), implied sorrow (Comp. Acts 21). And now, "on His knees," prostrate on the ground, prostrate on His Face, began His Agony. His very address bears witness to it. It is the only time, so far as recorded in the Gospels, when He addressed God with the personal pronoun: "My Father" (Matt. 26:39, 42).[22]

Christ was a "high priest of good things to come" (Hebrews 9:11). His authority was Divine and Eternal. The high priest appointed by men, Caiaphas, was blinded by corruption and could not see his Master. "There is a curious Jewish conceit, that on the Day of Atonement the golden band on the high Priest's mitre, with the graven words, 'Holiness unto Jehovah,' atoned for those who had blasphemed (Jer. Yoma 44c). It stands out in terrible contrast to the figure of Caiaphas on that awful night. Or did the unseen mitre on the True and Eternal High Priest's Brow, marking the consecration of His Humiliation to Jehovah, plead for them who in the night were gathered there, the blind leaders of the blind?"[23]

Christ was the high priest performing the final sacrifice: "For it is expedient that there should be a great and last sacrifice; yea, not a sacrifice of man, neither of beast, neither of any manner of foul; for it shall not be a human sacrifice; but it must be an infinite and eternal sacrifice" (Alma 34:10). His coat was "without seam, woven from the top throughout" (John 19:23). This was an inner garment, or *rabbinic kittuna*, only worn by the greatest religious teachers or priests of the temple.[24]

Edersheim's history of the life of Christ ends with a miracle as great as its beginning. For Edersheim, Jesus' miraculous birth and resurrection became parallel points in the life of Christ: "A dead Christ might have been a Teacher and Wonder-worker, and remembered and loved as such. But only a Risen and Living Christ could be the Saviour, the Life, and the Life-Giver—and as such preached to all men."[25] With his resurrection, he brought new life into the world as "the Second Adam, whose victory would restore what sin had lost; the true Son of God, God manifest in the flesh."[26]

# NOTES

1. Bleefeld and Shook, 202–3 (Talmudic Source: *Chulin* 59*b*).
2. Edersheim, *Tohu-va-Vohu*, 71.
3. Edersheim, *Life and Times*, 130.
4. Edersheim, *Life and Times*, 133.
5. Edersheim, *Sketches*, 76–78.
6. Millet, "The Birth and Childhood of the Messiah," 149; Edersheim, *Jesus the Messiah*, 146–47 (1:211–12).
7. Edersheim, *Jesus the Messiah*, 141 (1:203).
8. Edersheim, *Jesus the Messiah*, 142 (1:204).
9. Millet, "The Birth and Childhood of the Messiah," 149; Edersheim, *Jesus the Messiah*, 148–49 (1:214–15).
10. Edersheim, *Jesus the Messiah,* 149 (1:215).
11. Edersheim, *Jesus the Messiah*, 149 (1:215).
12. Edersheim, *Jesus the Messiah*, 247 (1:356).
13. Edersheim, *Jesus the Messiah*, 250 (1:362).
14. Edersheim, *Jesus the Messiah*, 250 (1:362).
15. Edersheim, *Jesus the Messiah*, 241 (1:351).
16. Edersheim, *Jesus the Messiah*, 250–51 (1:362–63).
17. Edersheim, *Jesus the Messiah*, 325 (1:468).
18. Edersheim, *Jesus the Messiah*, 325 (1:468).
19. Edersheim, *Jesus the Messiah*, 324 (1:467).
20. Edersheim, *Tohu-va-Vohu*, 97.
21. Edersheim, *Jesus the Messiah*, 846 (2:540).
22. Edersheim, *Jesus the Messiah*, 846 (2:540).
23. Edersheim, *Jesus the Messiah*, 861 (2:562).
24. Edersheim, *Temple*, 68.
25. Edersheim, *Jesus the Messiah*, 906 (2:629).
26. Edersheim, *Lectures*, 46.

# PART THREE

# THE LDS PERSPECTIVE

*"Our learned friend."*
—ELDER BRUCE R. McCONKIE

In this section, each of the most influential LDS authors who referenced Edersheim is discussed. The ideas presented by these LDS authors often extend beyond his perspective and give us respect for the power of continuing revelation in helping us gain a clearer understanding of the Bible and the divine mission of Jesus.

# Chapter Eleven

# The Latter-day Saints Meet Edersheim

It is not known when the first copy of Alfred Edersheim's *The Life and Times of Jesus the Messiah* arrived in Utah, but it could well be B. H. Roberts who brought it. Sent by the first presidency to Liverpool, Roberts was called to be the editor of the *Millennial Star* from 1886–87. Edersheim's works would have been widely accessible during this time in the libraries and bookstores in England. His first edition of *The Life and Times of Jesus the Messiah* was published in September of 1883. Because of its popularity, a second edition was published in March of 1886 with a third edition to follow shortly thereafter. His Warburton lectures were published in 1885, and the last of his volumes for *Bible History: Old Testament* was published in 1887.

EVEN THOUGH LDS missionaries were in England while he was alive, there is no information about Edersheim ever having met an LDS missionary or being introduced to the fulness of the gospel of Jesus Christ.

There is a feeling of "passing in the night" between Edersheim and the LDS missionaries in England. By 1887, Edersheim had left Torquay, his beloved parishioners, and St. Andrew's Cathedral for Bournemouth to change his religious affiliations and focus more on his writing. He started a new book on the life and writings of St. Paul at the encouragement of his publisher and had only written a few chapters when he caught a cold that went straight into his chest during the late fall of 1888. His doctor advised him to retire to Mentone, a health resort on the Italian Riviera, to enjoy a warmer winter. He quietly passed away there in the spring of the following year.

Even though he was born five years before the Church was organized and LDS missionaries were in England while he was alive, there is no information about Edersheim ever having met an LDS missionary or being introduced to the fulness of the gospel of Jesus Christ. Yet his writings indicate he had a yearning for a "universal" Christian church for all mankind without the turmoil of various Christian sects. Influenced by his Jewish upbringing, his personal beliefs—illustrated in his journal writing[1] about a separate, distinct godhead and a corporeal God—show a gospel understanding that went beyond the church to which he belonged.

Edersheim did gain some notoriety among biblical scholars of his day. It was during this time that B. H. Roberts spent much time in the Liverpool Picton Library researching archaeology and history for what was eventually his book *New Witnesses for God*. Edersheim's books would certainly have caught Robert's wide-ranging eye. Regardless of when he acquired it, *The Life and Times of Jesus the Messiah* is mentioned in Roberts's own journal as one of the important works Roberts studied in the late 1800s.[2] As a result of this study, he quoted Edersheim a dozen times in at least three of his books. B. H. Roberts's 1903 quotation of Alfred Edersheim's work was the first time the Jewish-Christian scholar was cited in an LDS work.

## EDERSHEIM'S STRENGTHS AS A RESOURCE

Since Roberts's first reference, Alfred Edersheim's works have continued to be quoted extensively[3] by a variety of LDS scholars and General Authorities in numerous publications. Many of these authors quote Edersheim in more than one publication, with most of these citations coming from three of Edersheim's works: *The Life and Times of Jesus the Messiah; The Temple: Its Ministry and Services;* and *Sketches of Jewish Social Life.* His explanations about Jewish customs, traditions, and the feasts and festivals of the temple all center on their symbolic significance in relation to the Savior. As members of his Church in the latter days, this emphasis on Jesus Christ throughout Edersheim's writings has struck a cord with LDS readers, scholars, and General Authorities in the past and continues today.

This does not answer the simple question of why LDS authors have referenced Edersheim so extensively, nor the more relevant query of whether his works are still pertinent or worthy of study. After review- ing the citations of LDS authors, there seems to be at least six reasons for Edersheim's profound influence; he is considered:

- An authority on the Septuagint, the Greek translation of the Old Testament used at the time of Christ.
- An expert linguist and translator.
- An authority on the Jews in Palestine at the time of Christ.
- An expert on Jewish traditions and customs.
- A commentator on Jewish doctrine clarifying LDS beliefs.
- A witness whose testimony of Jesus Christ, the Messiah, reso- nates with their own.

## AN AUTHORITY ON THE SEPTUAGINT

Edersheim studied Greek as a young man in the gymnasium and as a philosophy student at the university in Vienna. His study of Greek continued throughout his theological studies. Edersheim would have been taught Hebrew from his days at the synagogue school. Thus, he understood both Greek and Hebrew from the time he was a young boy. He also worked as a translator and obviously had a great facility for languages. His reading of the Septuagint (or LXX) would include an intrinsic understanding of the Hebrew scriptures from which the Septuagint was translated.

Because of his professional training, he was very aware of translation errors and saw the heavy Egyptian and Greek influences in the Septuagint. Since the Septuagint became the scriptures used and understood by most of the Jews during the time of Christ, these translation errors would promote misunderstandings of the original Hebrew. Edersheim pointed out "that this translation should be regarded by the Hellenists as inspired like the original."[4] B. H. Roberts found Edersheim's explanations about the Septuagint enlightening and used his commentary on the errors of the Septuagint in multiple publications.

## A LINGUIST AND TRANSLATOR

As already discussed, Edersheim had excellent training in languages and worked as a translator even as a young man. Many of his first publications were translations of religious works from other languages into English. In his own gospel commentaries, Edersheim would retranslate the Hebrew Old Testament or the Greek New Testament with a more accurate translation into English to help the reader understand specific words from another viewpoint. LDS authors sometimes used Edersheim's translations, including Elder Bruce R. McConkie, who referenced some of Edersheim's translations of the Hebrew prayers and psalms.[5]

For example, when a woman of Canaan came to the Savior asking for the healing of her daughter, the Savior seemed to answer her rather sharply: "It is not meet to take the children's bread, and to cast it to dogs" (Matthew 15:26). Edersheim translated the term *dogs* as meaning "little dogs" or "house dogs."[6] The woman replies, "Truth, Lord: yet the dogs eat of the crumbs which fall from their masters' table" (Matthew 15:27). This clarification makes better sense in defining the dogs as dogs within the household who are under the table. They do not have the same privileges as the children sitting at the table, but they are still given food by the Master of all: "Heathenism may be like the dogs, when compared with the children's place and privileges; but He is their Master still, and they under His table; and when He breaks the bread there is enough and to spare for them—even under the table they eat of the children's crumbs."[7]

## AN AUTHORITY ON THE JEWS

Edersheim studied much of the historical source documents that were available to him during his time. He studied Josephus's writings and other Roman histories written during the time of Christ. His background in Jewish religious traditions gave him a deeper understanding of the historical context and nuances between the various people involved during Jesus' lifetime. He also studied the best criticisms and gospel commentaries of his day both in English and German. In addition, he used "such kindred studies as those of Biblical geography and antiquities and the Egyptian and Assyrian monuments,"[8] which he probably found in the British Museum. As a scholar of Eastern studies, he came to the conclusion that the more one studies ancient history, the more one is struck with the end result of Christianity for the world. It was the deliverance of the individual—"the acknowledgment of individuality, of individual dignity, of moral individuality, and of individual liberty."[9] Edersheim saw Christianity and the teachings of Christ as laying the foundation for modern society in its loftiest and noblest aspirations.

His historical insights about Annas, the high priest, were used by Elder Talmage in *Jesus the Christ* and by other authors.[10] Annas had been the appointed high priest by the Roman government for only six or seven years, but his influence would be felt in Jerusalem for his entire lifetime. At least five of his sons, a grandson, and his son-in-law, Caiaphas, became high priests. His immense fortune and worldly wealth was inextricably connected with the temple booths and the selling of animals for sacrifice: "We have seen what immense revenues the family of Annas must have derived from the Temple booths, and how nefarious and unpopular was the traffic. The names of those bold, licentious, unscrupulous, degenerate sons of Aaron were spoken with whispered curses. Without referring to Christ's interference with that Temple-traffic, which, if His authority had prevailed, would of course have been fatal to it, we can understand how antithetic in every respect a Messiah, and such a Messiah as Jesus, must have been to Annas."[11]

## AN EXPERT ON JEWISH TRADITIONS

Edersheim studied the Targumim, the Midrash, and the Jerusalem and Babylonian Talmud for greater understanding of the traditions of the Jewish people. Even though many of these documents were written centuries after Christ's lifetime, Edersheim realized that the strict oral tradition of the rabbis and priests kept most of these traditions very similar. The biggest difference was Jewish worship without the temple in Jerusalem. As a young Jewish boy from an orthodox home, he would have experienced many of the same traditions of young Jewish boys at the time of Christ (wearing a tzitzit, the tallit, and tephillin, especially at his own bar mitzvah). He was taught about these traditions and customs and lived them. After gaining his testimony of Jesus as the Messiah, he was able to see the Savior in all the traditions and customs of his youth. His commentary on Jewish traditions and customs and their fulfillment in Christ is the area of expertise most sought after by LDS writers.

The presentation of the first fruits was just such a tradition. It would have a powerful effect on a Jewish family. All families in Israel would participate. This tradition taught all within the home how the Lord's bounty comes first. As spring turned into early summer, the first ripening fruits would appear both on the ground and on the trees.

> The head of the family . . . accompanied by his child, would go into his field and mark off certain portions from among the most promising of the crop. For only the best might be presented to the Lord, and it was set apart before it was yet ripe, and solemn dedication being, however, afterwards renewed, when it was actually cut. Thus, each time any one would go into the field, he would be reminded of the ownership of Jehovah, till the reapers cut down the golden harvest.[12]

This tradition of dedicating their best or first fruits to the Lord taught the Jews how the Lord should be first in all aspects of their lives. As they gave him their best, the Lord in return would make them his first fruits during the resurrection. Those who rise in the morning of the first resurrection are "Christ's, the first fruits, they who shall descend with him first, and they who are on the earth and in their graves, who are first caught up to meet him; and all this by the voice of the sounding of the trump of the angel of God" (D&C 88:98).

## CLARIFYING LDS BELIEFS

Even though Edersheim was a paid minister of the Church of England and was compelled to publicly espouse certain stances of doctrine, there are clear excerpts in his writings that point to his frustrations with church questions: "There are people who express themselves with such elaborate distinctness as to become at last indistinct, repeating and re-repeating till they succeed in bamboozling themselves and every other person."[13]

"Why are preachers in the habit of asking a series of questions in the pulpit when they immediately add: 'These are questions which we cannot answer'? What can be the use of publicly asking a question which on your own showing you cannot answer?"[14]

"Our religious differences mostly spring from what all of us do not know, but pretend to know."[15]

His conversion to Christianity and changing to another Christian sect was based on his quest for truth. He was not blinded by the religious customs of his birth and upbringing. Instead, he was willing to completely change for the truth. This showed his humility and understanding of truth at a deeper level. He realized that seeking and learning truth was an ongoing process: "Thank God for what He reveals and thank God for what He conceals. The faith which follows God into the light is supplemented and completed by that which follows Him in the dark."[16]

Through his writings, Edersheim tried to find the light by following God into the darkness with faith. He was able to seek for truth beyond the confines of his religion. President Joseph Fielding Smith realized this additional understanding when he quoted Edersheim in general conference.

## A WITNESS OF JESUS CHRIST

Leaving Judaism and embracing Christ was a difficult, life-changing decision. Similar to the early Jewish Christians of the New Testament, Edersheim's conversion to Christianity meant establishing new religious traditions and beliefs, plus new associations and relationships with others. Because of his decision to become a Christian, Edersheim's life would be completely altered. His inner life changed as well, and he became a new man.

Edersheim experienced many trials in his life, such as years of bad health, persecution, and the death of a loved one. These times of adversity did not jeopardize his conversion to Christianity, but intensified his faith in Jesus Christ. He wrote, "Ours it is now only to 'believe,' where we cannot further know, and, looking up to the Son of Man in

His perfected work, to perceive, and to receive the gift of God's love for our healing."[17]

In a world torn apart because of misunderstandings between the sons of Abraham, Jesus Christ is the instrument through which the covenant can be realized for all nations and people, and Edersheim's words lend a healing balm to salve those spiritual wounds. He is a "learned friend" who helps us understand the historical Old and New Testament contexts for these worldwide conflicts. Edersheim wrote, "The Lord Jesus Christ, [is] the one Prophet, the one Priest, the one King, that in Him the kingdom of heaven might be opened to all believers, and from Him the blessings of salvation flow unto all men."[18]

Edersheim's testimony is simple yet powerful. He understood the personal relationship each person must develop with the Savior and the effects that relationship would have on a person's soul:

> Faith in God makes us optimists; experience of the world and of men, pessimists. Can we be both at the same time? Yes, by renouncing the world.[19]

> I believe in a personal God; I also believe in a personal Satan. Agnosticism on the latter point seems to me to lay us open to the most serious practical dangers.[20]

> I am devoutly thankful to God for every evidence in favour of Christianity. Each is a joyous discovery.[21]

Edersheim's works are still valid today because of this testimony of Jesus Christ, the Messiah and Savior of the world. By preserving and revealing the symbolism behind the cultural and religious customs of the Israelites, Edersheim uncovered the powerful context of sacred traditions and events. Edersheim testified, "Christ is indeed the end of the Law for righteousness, to Whom all the ordinances of the Old Testament had pointed, and in Whom alone, alike the people and the history of Israel, find their meaning."[22] We are indebted to Alfred Edersheim for his clarifying illustrations of the link between ancient practices and their fulfillment in Jesus Christ, his historical backgrounds for understanding the Old and New Testament, and his linguistic explanations and translations. Often, these will further clarify our own LDS beliefs about the Savior.

# NOTES

1. Edersheim wrote in his journal, "I am convinced of the historical Church; I believe in a national Church; I prefer a liturgical Church and on these grounds I have joined the Church of England" (*Tohu-va-Vohu*, 45). "With reverence be it said: Our modern theology has almost lost sight of the Father. Our thoughts and our prayers are almost exclusively directed to the Second Person of the Godhead. Yet it is to the Father we are to come through the Son and by the Holy Spirit; and it was the object of the Son to reveal the Father, through the Holy Spirit given unto us" (*Tohu-va-Vohu*, 14).

2. Madsen, *Defender of the Faith*, 84.

3. As pointed out in chapter 1, there are hundreds of Edersheim citations included in a variety of LDS works.

4. Edersheim, *Jesus the Messiah*, 20 (1:29).

5. McConkie, *The Mortal Messiah*, 3:136; Edersheim, *Jesus the Messiah*, 584 (2:160).

6. Edersheim, *Jesus the Messiah*, footnote 5, 502 (2:41). Elder Talmage also quotes Edersheim's translation in *Jesus the Christ*, 340.

7. Edersheim, *Jesus the Messiah*, 503 (2:44).

8. Edersheim, *Bible History*, 3.

9. Edersheim, *Tohu-va-Vohu*, 87. Edersheim, *Jesus the Messiah*, 3–75 (1:3–107). The first section of this book is titled "The Jewish World in the Days of Christ."

10. Talmage, *Jesus the Christ*, 597. Also, Ludlow, *A Companion to your Study of Doctrine and Covenants*, 2:431, uses the same Edersheim quote.

11. Edersheim, *Jesus the Messiah*, 2:547–48; as quoted by Talmage, *Jesus the Christ*, 525.

12. McConkie and Millet, *Doctrinal Commentary on the Book of Mormon*, 2:42; Edersheim, *The Temple*, 380–81.

13. Edersheim, *Tohu-va-Vohu*, 21.

14. Edersheim, *Tohu-va-Vohu*, 83.

15. Edersheim, *Tohu-va-Vohu*, 10.

16. Edersheim, *Tohu-va-Vohu*, 22.

17. Edersheim, *Jesus the Messiah*, 268 (1:388).

18. Edersheim, *Bible History*, 10.

19. Edersheim, *Tohu-va-Vohu*, 126.

20. Edersheim, *Tohu-va-Vohu*, 85.

21, Edersheim, *Tohu-va-Vohu*, 28.

22. Edersheim, *Temple*, viii.

# CHAPTER TWELVE

# B. H. ROBERTS:
# EDERSHEIM ARRIVES IN UTAH

B. H. ROBERTS WAS A voracious reader and biblical scholar. He studied a wide variety of scriptural commentaries, which he listed in his journal. Included in the long list of books he used for his research were Alfred Edersheim's *The Life and Times of Jesus the Messiah* and a book written by Edersheim's professor in Germany, Johann August Neander, entitled *The Christian Religion and Church.*[1] Roberts would quote Edersheim in at least three of his works.

## THE FIRST REFERENCE TO EDERSHEIM

In 1903, B. H. Roberts first quoted Edersheim in his book *The Mormon Doctrine of Deity.* This was the first time the Jewish Christian scholar was cited in any LDS work. The purpose of this book was to answer Protestant and Catholic questions about the LDS view of God as a corporeal being. Truman Madsen in his biography on B. H. Roberts gives us some interesting background:

> In the winter of 1901, two Salt Lake City Protestant ministers gave a series of lectures on the Protestant understanding of God and directed much of their polemic against Mormon theism. Roberts

delivered a response at a youth conference, entitled *The Mormon View of Deity*, which expanded on his conviction: "I can see in this doctrine of God the highest spirituality of which man is capable." Roberts confronted the metaphysical God of the ancient creeds with the biblical personalism enhanced by modern revelation.[2]

B. H. Roberts had a similar debate with Cyril Van Der Donckt, a Roman Catholic Jesuit priest who charged that "the Latter-day Saint understanding and experience of God was 'awful blasphemy,' 'soul destroying,' 'the lowest kind of materialism,' 'destructive of all truly religious sentiment,' the 'crudest possible conception of God,' 'absolutely incompatible with spirituality,' and 'worse than the basest forms of idolatry.' "[3] Roberts's response to these attacks was based on his knowledge of the scriptures, his reading of Greek and Hebrew philosophers, and his understanding of the issue through the restored gospel of Jesus Christ. He bore a strong testimony that the conception of God as a being without body, parts, or passions had "its origin in Greek philosophy and not in Jewish or Christian revelation."[4]

This point is clearly illustrated in the New Testament when Phillip asked the Savior: "Lord, shew us the Father, and it sufficeth us. Jesus saith unto him, Have I been so long time with you, and yet hast thou not known me, Philip? He that hath seen me hath seen the Father" (John 14:8–9).

In *The Mormon Doctrine of Deity*, Roberts refuted the current attack of other religionists against the LDS Church's view on the being of God. He bore a strong witness that "Jesus is God in his own right and person and he is a revelation of what God the Father is. He is not only a revelation of the being of God, but of the *kind* of being God is. . . . It is becoming in man to accept with humility what God has been pleased to reveal concerning his own nature, being assured that in God's infinite knowledge he knows himself, and that which he reveals concerning himself is to be trusted far beyond man's philosophical conception of him."[5]

Roberts felt the Greek philosophical traditions that took the early Christians away from the true nature of God were already corrupting the Jews during the time of Christ. Their view of God was being tainted by heathen beliefs through Jewish Greek philosophers. Both Roberts and Edersheim felt that the Septuagint, or Greek translation, of the Hebrew Bible had been translated in a way to change the view of Deity and the scriptures as the word of God. Roberts used the famous philosopher Aristobolus as an example of someone who mixed Greek thought with Jewish doctrine. Aristobolus was a Hellenistic Jewish philosopher who lived in Alexandria in the middle of the second century BC. He interpreted the Mosaic law's teachings about Jehovah in the Septuagint as being similar to Greek philosophical traditions of Deity.[6] The Greeks believed in the pluralism of gods and in gods who could take the shape of man. Roberts realized the permeating influence of Greek rationalism and the traditions of Plato and Aristotle were having an effect on the doctrines of Deity. Even for the Jew, these beliefs were becoming more Greek than Hebrew.

Roberts discussed the fact that there were many who were anxious to place such a pagan structure on the scriptures. Aristobolus argued that the whole order of the world taught by Aristotle could be found in the Bible. Roberts quoted Edersheim to refute Aristobolus's assertion that the Bible came from Greek philosophical traditions rather than the other way around. Edersheim saw "the mighty spell which Greek philosophy exercised on all kindred minds and the special adaptation of the Jewish intellect to such subtle, if not deep thinking."[7] Edersheim refuted such allegations that Greek philosophy was the basis for the law: "Of course, the Bible had not learned from Aristotle, but he and all other philosophers had learned from the Bible. Thus, according to Aristobolus, Pythagoras, Plato, and all the other sages, had really learned from Moses, and the broken rays found in their writings were united in all their glory in the Torah."[8]

## TRANSLATION ERRORS OF THE OLD TESTAMENT

Later in this same book, Roberts discussed the character of the Septuagint translation, citing Edersheim as an authoritative linguist and translator on the topic. In a long citation, Edersheim discussed the use of Egyptian words, plus distinctive Grecian elements in this important Greek translation of the Old Testament. Edersheim felt the Alexandrian translators had divested "abstract truth of its concrete, national, Judaistic envelope."[9] Edersheim concluded his analysis of the Greek translation as follows:

> Putting aside clerical mistakes and misreadings, and making allowance for errors of translation, ignorance, and haste, we note certain outstanding facts as characteristic of the Greek version. . . . By the side of slavish and false literalism there is great liberty, if not license, in handling the original; gross mistakes occur along with happy renderings of very difficult passages, suggesting the aid of some able scholars.[10]

As an able scholar himself, Edersheim understood the difficulties of translation. He worked professionally as a translator with his initial religious publications being English translations of gospel works in other languages.[11] He was fluent in at least seven languages, including Greek and Hebrew.[12] He understood the importance of being true to the original text. Acknowledging the great work done by the legendary seventy plus translators of the Septuagint, he was still concerned that some of the "highest truths" might have been sacrificed through the translation of these sacred words. Through the Prophet Joseph Smith, we voice a similar view every time we recite the eighth article of faith. It states in part, "We believe the Bible to be the word of God as far as it is translated correctly."

Roberts discussed the corruption of the Bible translation stemming from the changes made by the Septuagint translators. He referenced Nephi's own prophecy concerning the corruption of the Bible: "Wherefore, thou seest that after the book hath gone forth through the hands of the great and abominable church, that there are many plain and precious things taken away from the book, which is the book of the Lamb of God" (1 Nephi 13:28). Roberts argued that Nephi might be pointing to the apostate Jewish church as having contributed to taking out some of the "plain and precious things" of the scriptures:

> It may be urged, with reference to the Old Testament at least, that it came from the Jews to the Gentiles in its present form, and that it was not the Gentiles, not the apostate church of the third and fourth century of the Christian era that mutilated in any form the Old Testament scriptures. But let us not take too narrow a view of Nephi's vision-prophecy, concerning the corruption of the word of God, or the power which he saw corrupting it. It may be that he had in mind in his vision as much the apostate Jewish church as the apostate Christian church, and looking upon the question from that view point we know this: that a century or two before the advent of Christ the Jews apparently had grown weary of the honorable

mission which God had given to them; namely, that of being his witnesses among the nations of the earth; and their leading teachers, especially in the two centuries preceding the coming of the Messiah, were taking every step that their ingenuity could devise for harmonizing the truths which God had made known to them with the more fashionable conceptions of God as entertained by one or the other of the great sects of philosophy among the Romans.[13]

To further this point, Roberts quotes Edersheim as stating that the Septuagint became the people's Bible and was considered inspired like the original Hebrew scriptures: "It was part of the case that this translation should be regarded by the Hellenists as inspired like the original."[14] Stemming from his experience as a translator, Edersheim worried about the Jew's interpretation of every shade of meaning of the Greek words in the Septuagint: "Even more extravagant was the idea that a word which occurred in the Septuagint might be interpreted according to every shade of meaning which it bore in the Greek, and that even another meaning might be given it by slightly altering the letters."[15] Edersheim realized that the translation would not have the power and meaning of the original Hebrew words.

Roberts later quoted these same Edersheim passages in his books *New Witnesses for God*[16] and *The Truth, The Way, The Life*[17] about the Septuagint, the errors in its translation, the Greek and Egyptian influences, and the use of the Septuagint by the Jews. These statements of Edersheim support a recurring theme in Roberts's books refuting the false philosophies of the world in regards to the nature of God and false interpretations of the scriptures.

## INAPPROPRIATE CRITICISM

In *Defense of the Faith and the Saints* (1907), Roberts wrote a treatise defending the Church against the critics of his day. He was particularly frustrated by critics who took statements of Church leaders out of context or used quotes when Church authorities were simply voicing their opinions rather than speaking inspired words as prophets. Roberts wrote, "It cannot be that the world is so ignorant in this enlightened age as not to know that churches cannot be held responsible for every utterance that is made in their name and from their pulpits."[18] Then, he quotes "learned" Edersheim: "No one would measure the belief of

Christians by certain statements in the Fathers; nor judge the moral principles of Roman Catholics, by prurient quotations from the casuists; nor yet estimate Lutherans by the utterances and deeds of the early successors of Luther; nor Calvinists by the burning of Servitus. In all such cases the general standpoint of the times has to be first taken into account."[19] Roberts brings Edersheim's thought into the context of the LDS Church and church leaders: "So it is in our history, not every word that has been spoken, even by men high in authority in the Church, has always been the exact and perfect word of God."[20]

"OUR SEVENTIES SHOULD KNOW
what so high an authority, as Edersheim is generally accepted to be, has said upon the subject."
—B. H. Roberts

## SO HIGH AN AUTHORITY

It is important to note that Roberts did not always agree with Edersheim. In *The Seventy's Course in Theology* (1907–1912), Roberts took issue with Edersheim on his views on the calling of the Seventy in the New Testament. In Luke 10:1, the Savior "appointed other seventy also, and sent them two and two before his face into every city and place, whither he himself would come." In his discussion of this scripture, Edersheim compared the calling of a seventy to the calling of an Apostle. The Apostles were called for life, but "no power or authority was formally conferred on the Seventy, their mission being only temporary, and indeed, for one definite purpose; its primary object was to prepare for the coming of the Master in the places to which they were sent; and their selection was from the wider circle of disciples, the number being now Seventy instead of Twelve."[21]

Roberts, on the other hand, felt that Edersheim was "in the main, wrong in his treatment of this subject of the Seventy."[22] He regarded the Seventy as permanent officers in the Church, based on the Church practices of his day. Interestingly, the calling of the Seventy today has gone through some changes in the LDS Church. There are still General Authorities who are called to the First Quorum of the Seventy for a lifelong calling. Yet other men who are called as Seventies are only given the calling for a specified length of time as "traveling ministers, unto the Gentiles first and also unto the Jews" (D&C 107:97), similar to Edersheim's description.

In spite of these divergent views, Roberts demonstrated his high respect for Edersheim when he noted in the footnote to this section that, even though he disagreed with him, he felt, "our Seventies should know what so high an authority, as Edersheim is generally accepted to be, has said upon the subject." [23]

# NOTES

1. Madsen, *Defender of the Faith*, 84.
2. Madsen, *Defender of the Faith*, 289.
3. Madsen, *Defender of the Faith*, 289.
4. Madsen, *Defender of the Faith*, 290.
5. Roberts, *The Mormon Doctrine of Deity*, 119–20.
6. Roberts, *The Mormon Doctrine of Deity*, 119–20.
7. Roberts, *The Mormon Doctrine of Deity*, 179–81.
8. Edersheim, *Jesus the Messiah*, 25 (1:36).
9. Roberts, *The Mormon Doctrine of Deity*, 181–82; Edersheim, *Jesus the Messiah*, 1:29, 19–20. Roberts initiated the citation: "Following is a sample, according to Edersheim, of his [meaning Aristobolus's] allegorizing: 'Thus when we read that God stood, it meant the stable order of the world; that he created the world in six days, the orderly succession of time; the rest of the Sabbath, the preservation of what was created. And in such manner could the whole system of Aristotle be found in the Bible. But how was this to be accounted for?' "
10. Edersheim, *Jesus the Messiah*, 25 (1:36).
11. Roberts, *The Mormon Doctrine of Deity*, 180–81; Edersheim's *Jesus the Messiah*, 19–21 (1:27–28). Many of Edersheim's publications (especially his initial works) were translations of German and Latin texts. Some of them include: Edersheim, *The Jubilee Rhythm of St. Bernard of Clairvaux on the Name of Jesus and Other Hymns*, a collection of Latin hymns translated by Edersheim; H. M. Chalybaeus, *Historical Development of Speculative Philosophy from 1854: Kant to Hegel*, translated by Edersheim from German; Kurts, *History of the Old Covenant*, translated by Edersheim from German.

12. Mayhew, "Alfred Edersheim: A Brief Biography," 171. Mayhew speculated that Edersheim was fluent in the languages of German, French, English, Hebrew, Latin, Greek, and Dutch. In *Tohu-va-Vohu*, Edersheim's daughter Ella also mentioned Edersheim's facility with languages, describing his "linguistic attainments" (xi).

13. Roberts, *The Mormon Doctrine of Deity*, 179–80.

14. Roberts, *The Mormon Doctrine of Deity*, 181; Edersheim, *Jesus the Messiah*, 20 (1:29).

15. Roberts, *The Mormon Doctrine of Deity*, 183.

16. Roberts, *New Witnesses for God*, 3:269–72.

17. Roberts, *The Truth, The Way, The Life*, 173.

18. Roberts, *Defense of the Faith and the Saints*, 2:455.

19. Roberts, *Defense of the Faith and the Saints*, 2:455.

20. Roberts, *Defense of the Faith and the Saints*, 2:455.

21. Roberts, *Seventy's Course in Theology*, 1:3; Edersheim, *Jesus the Messiah*, 567 (2:136).

22. Roberts, *Seventy's Course in Theology*, 1:3; Edersheim, *Jesus the Messiah*, 567 (2:136).

23. Roberts, *Seventy's Course in Theology*, 1:3. Roberts began the footnote with this commentary: "Such references [Edersheim's *Jesus the Messiah*] are made that the student may consult the literature on a given point. He must make his own deductions as to the correctness of the statements and arguments of such authors."

# Chapter Thirteen

# James E. Talmage: Introducing Edersheim to a Larger Audience

Although B. H. Roberts was the first to quote Edersheim to an LDS audience, it was Elder James E. Talmage who brought him to the attention of the larger Church membership. In his master work, *Jesus the Christ,* written between 1908 and 1915, Talmage cited Edersheim at least twenty-three times,[1] often at great length. Called to the Quorum of the Twelve during the writing of this book, Talmage finished its pages in the Salt Lake Temple.[2] His copy of *The Life and Times of Jesus the Messiah* was the only one of Edersheim's books used as a reference, along with other works of biblical scholars, to "reflect a conscious effort to explore ideas by men of faith, men who believed in the existence of God in an era when skeptical criticism abounded."[3]

Edersheim also felt surrounded by "skeptical criticism," but his optimistic spirit saw the fruits of religious conflict as bringing people closer to the truth: "And so every controversy, however bitter or threatening in its course, ultimately contributes to the establishment of truth—not merely, nor even principally, by the answer to objections which it calls forth, but by the fuller consideration of what had been invalidated, and the consequent wider and more accurate understanding of it. Thus, long after the din of controversy has ceased, . . . the peaceful fruits of the contest remain as a permanent gain."[4]

Edersheim and Talmage were in England at the same time, even though they never met. In 1862, Talmage was born in Berkshire, England. This is the same year Edersheim moved to England from Scotland. As a young teenage boy, Talmage and his family met some LDS missionaries and joined the Church. In 1876, the entire family left England for America to join the Saints in Utah. This is the same year Edersheim published his book *Sketches of Jewish Social Life in the Days of Christ*.

Elder Talmage was a science professor in chemistry and geology and a university administrator serving as president of the University of Utah. Similar to B. H. Roberts, he was a great reader of religious books and scriptural commentaries. Though it is not known if B. H. Roberts actually introduced Elder Talmage to Edersheim, they were contemporaries and served in high administrative Church callings during the same period of time. Roberts's first book quoting Edersheim was published five years before Talmage started writing *Jesus the Christ*.

## CLARIFYING THE CONTEXT OF SCRIPTURE

In Edersheim's works, he preserves and communicates the cultural and religious customs of the Israelites, revealing the powerful context of these events in their fulfillment in Jesus Christ. Talmage cites Edersheim in relation to these Jewish customs and practices. For example, during the Feast of Tabernacles, the Savior declared himself the Living Water (John 7:37–38) and the Light of the World (John 8:12) in direct fulfillment of the two most important ceremonies of the feast, which were "the pouring out of water and the illumination of the Temple."[5]

Many other examples of these references used by Talmage have already been discussed in detail in previous chapters, such as:

- The use of Targumim in the synagogue;
- The term "friend of the bridegroom" used in Judea but not Galilee;
- The parting of the ways of the disciples of Christ after his Bread of Life sermon;
- The term *little dogs* or *house dogs* as referring to the heathen;
- Annas as a well-known historical figure;
- The illegalities of the Jewish trial of Jesus;
- And the Jews crying, "We have no King but Caesar," causing generations of judgment on the Jewish people.

# THE USE OF PARABLES

Elder Talmage also quoted Edersheim to explain possible reasons for Jesus' use of parables and to clarify the meaning of the symbols within them. During the time of Christ, the Jews used parables as a common way of teaching, yet Jesus' parables gave spiritual insight to those who were ready to receive it. Edersheim wrote, "Perhaps no other mode of teaching was so common among the Jews as that by parables. Only in their case, they were almost entirely illustrations of what had been said or taught; while in the case of Christ, they served as the foundation for His teaching. . . . In the one case it was intended to make spiritual teaching appear Jewish and national, in the other to convey spiritual teaching in a new form adapted to the stand-point of the hearers."[6]

The lessons of Jesus' parables were only understood through study and prayer: "Who hath ears to hear, let him hear" (Matthew 13:9). For those unwilling to listen, his parables were difficult to understand. Talmage wrote, "There is plainly shown an element of mercy in the parabolic mode of instruction adopted by our Lord under the conditions prevailing at the time. Had He always taught in explicit declaration, such as required no interpretation, many among His hearers would have come under condemnation, inasmuch as they were too weak in faith and unprepared in heart to break the bonds of traditionalism and the prejudice engendered by sin, as to accept and obey the saving word."[7]

# TREASURE HID IN A FIELD

There are multiple parables the Savior taught about the nature of the kingdom of heaven. For many of these, Talmage used Edersheim's commentary to further clarify their meaning. One parable was about hidden treasure accidentally found in a field: "The kingdom of heaven is like unto treasure hid in a field; the which when a man hath found, he hideth, and for joy thereof goeth and selleth all that he hath, and buyeth that field" (Matthew 13:44). After the man discovers the prize, he gives all that he has to gain its possession. Some have criticized this parable as promoting illegal or unethical behavior by not disclosing the discovery of the riches to the rightful owner of the field.

In Jesus' time, finding concealed treasure was not uncommon. Because of the threat of thieves and civil unrest for generations, many Jews had hidden their valuables. Under Jewish law, claiming treasure that was not yours was not considered dishonest. Edersheim explained, "It was, at least, in entire accordance with Jewish law. If a man had found a treasure in loose coins among the corn it would certainly be his if he bought the corn. If he had found it on the ground, or in the soil, it would equally certainly belong to him if he could claim owner- ship of the soil, and even if the field were not his own, unless others could prove their right to it. The law went so far as to adjudge to the purchaser of fruits anything found among fruits."[8] Talmage indicated the Savior was teaching by this illustration "once the treasure of the kingdom is found, the finder should lose no time nor shrink from any sacrifice needful to [e]nsure his title thereto."[9]

## THE EYE OF A NEEDLE

A rich young ruler had come to the Savior asking him, "What lack I yet?" (Matthew 19:20). The Savior told the young man to "sell that thou hast, and give to the poor, and thou shalt have treasure in heaven: and come and follow me" (Matthew 19:21), but the young man would not do it and went away sorrowful. After the man left, the Savior com- mented to his disciples that it would be "easier for a camel to go through the eye of a needle, than for a rich man to enter into the kingdom of God" (Matthew 19:24). His disciples were amazed by this statement and asked, "Who then can be saved?" (Matthew 19:25).

Talmage used a quote by Edersheim to illustrate that this saying of the Savior about the camel and the needle's eye was familiar to those who heard the remark. Edersheim wrote that there was a "common Jewish proverb, that a man did not even in his dreams see an elephant pass through the eye of a needle."[10] Talmage also pointed out that the needle's eye was applied to a small door or wicket set in the walls of the cities which was very difficult for a camel to squeeze through without being unloaded and stripped of all its costly burden.

Jesus was teaching his disciples that wealth is a temptation, but not an insurmountable barrier barring the entrance to the kingdom of God. The rich young ruler had been given a test to see if he could resist the temptation of riches and move past this obstacle. Talmage stated,

"Willingness to place the kingdom of God above all material possessions was the one thing he lacked. Every one of us may pertinently ask,
What do I lack?"[11]

## LABORERS IN THE VINEYARD

In the parable of the laborers, a master of a vineyard sets out early
in the morning to hire laborers. He agrees to pay the laborers a penny a
day. Throughout the day, even up until the last hour, additional laborers come into the vineyard to help work. At the end of the day the
master of the vineyard pays them all a penny. The laborers who had
worked all day long complained that they received the same wages as
those who only worked an hour, for "these last have wrought but one
hour, and thou hast made them equal unto us, which have borne the
burden and heat of the day" (Matthew 20:12). The master of the vineyard answered, "Friend, I do thee no wrong: didst not thou agree with
me for a penny? . . . Is it not lawful for me to do what I will with mine
own?" (Matthew 20:13, 15).

Talmage puts this parable in context. Peter had recently asked
the question: "What shall we have therefore?" (Matthew 19:27). The
Savior does not rebuke Peter for having an undue concern about his
wages; instead he lovingly teaches him a lesson, giving this parable to
Peter and the other disciples in answer to this question. Then, Talmage
quotes Edersheim describing the Savior's concern for his followers with
their questions of "What's in it for me?":

> There was here deep danger to the disciples: danger of lapsing
> into feelings akin to those with which the Pharisees viewed the par-
> doned publicans, . . . danger of misunderstanding the right relations,
> and with it the very character of the kingdom, and of work in and for
> it. . . . The principle which Christ lays down is, that, while nothing
> done for Him shall lose its reward, yet, from one reason or another,
> no forecast can be made, no inferences of self-righteousness may be
> drawn. It does not by any means follow, that more work done—at
> least to our seeing and judging—shall entail a greater reward. . . .
> Spiritual pride and self assertion can only be the outcome either of
> misunderstanding God's relation to us, or else of a wrong state of
> mind towards others. . . . But, while illustrating how it may come
> that some who were first are last, and how utterly mistaken or wrong
> is the thought that they must necessarily receive more than others,

who seemingly, have done more—how, in short, work for Christ is not a ponderable quantity, so much for so much, nor yet we be the judges of when and why a worker has come—it also conveys much that is new, and in many respects, most comforting.[12]

After this quote, Talmage wrote, "The Master shall judge as to the desserts of each servant; the wage at best is a free gift; for on the basis of strict accounting who of us is not in debt to God?"[13]

## THE MUSTARD SEED

In Matthew 13:31, Jesus taught the parable of the mustard seed: "The kingdom of heaven is like to a grain of mustard seed, which a man took and sowed in his field: which indeed is the least of all seeds: but when it is grown, it is the greatest among herbs and becometh a tree, so that the birds of the air come and lodge in the branches thereof." In the chapter note, Talmage quoted Edersheim's explanation of the grown mustard plant:

> Indeed, it looks no longer like a large garden-herb or shrub, but "becomes" or rather appears like "a tree"—as St. Luke puts it, "a great tree," of course, not in comparison with other trees, but with garden-shrubs. Such growth of mustard seed was also a fact well known at the time, and, indeed, still observed in the East. . . . And the general meaning would the more easily be apprehended, that a tree, whose wide-spreading branches afforded lodgment to the birds of heaven, was a familiar Old Testament figure for a mighty kingdom that gave shelter to the nations (Ezek. 31:6, 12; Dan. 4:12, 14, 21, 22). Indeed, it is specifically used as an illustration of the Messianic Kingdom (Ezek. 17:23).[14]

Edersheim makes reference to Ezekiel's and Daniel's visions of the messianic kingdom filling the earth and giving shelter to all nations. Daniel wrote about his dream, "Thus were the visions of mine head in my bed; I saw, and behold a tree in the midst of the earth . . . and the height thereof reached unto heaven, and the sight thereof to the end of all the earth: the leaves thereof were fair and the fruit thereof much . . . and the fowls of the heaven dwelt in the boughs thereof, and all flesh was fed of it" (Daniel 4:10–12). Ezekiel's vision is similar: "In the mountain of the height of Israel will I plant it: and it shall bring forth boughs, and bear fruit, and be a goodly cedar: and under it shall dwell all fowl of every wing; in the shadow of the branches thereof shall they dwell" (Ezekiel 17:23).

The Jews would be familiar with these images from the books of Daniel and Ezekiel and would understand the Savior's reference to them. Through the symbol of the mustard seed turning into a tree, Jesus was declaring his mission as starting the great messianic kingdom, and that he was indeed the Messiah.

Although he wrote other books,[15] *Jesus the Christ* was the only one in which Talmage referenced Edersheim, primarily due to its subject matter. The respect Talmage had for Edersheim's scholarship and understanding of Jesus the Messiah is evident when reviewing all of the Edersheim quotations in *Jesus the Christ* (a complete list is included in the appendix). It is clear that Talmage referenced Edersheim in every aspect of the Savior's life. Through Talmage's chapter notes, many LDS readers have gained a love of Edersheim, sometimes without even realizing it.

# NOTES

1. Talmage, *Jesus the Christ*, 160, 174, 188, 202, 281–82, 323, 341, 347, 391, 451, 504, 526, 573, 597–99, 601, 619, 649. See Table 2 in the appendix. The 1983 edition of *Jesus the Christ* is the one used for page numbers unless otherwise specified.
2. Talmage, *Jesus the Christ*, xi.
3. Talmage, *Jesus the Christ*, xii.
4. Edersheim, *Lectures*, viii.
5. Edersheim, *The Temple*, 227.
6. Talmage, *Jesus the Christ*, chapter 19, note 9; Edersheim, *Jesus the Messiah*, 401–2 (1:580–81).
7. Talmage, *Jesus the Christ*, chapter 19, 296 (1974 edition).
8. Talmage, *Jesus the Christ*, chapter 19, note 8.
9. Talmage, *Jesus the Christ*, 292 (1974 edition).
10. Talmage, *Jesus the Christ*, chapter 27, note 7.
11. Talmage, *Jesus the Christ*, 478 (1974 edition).
12. Talmage, *Jesus the Christ*, chapter 27, note 8.
13. Talmage, *Jesus the Christ*, 482 (1974 edition).
14. Talmage, *Jesus the Christ*, 280; Edersheim, *Jesus the Messiah*, 408–9 (1:593).
15. Talmage did write other books, such as *The Articles of Faith*, *The Great Apostasy*, *Vitality of Mormonism*, and *The House of the Lord*, but he did not quote Edersheim in his other works.

# CHAPTER FOURTEEN

# JOSEPH FIELDING SMITH: QUOTING EDERSHEIM AT GENERAL CONFERENCE

As a member of the Council of the Twelve, Elder Joseph Fielding Smith served with Elder James E. Talmage. He had read *Jesus the Christ* and was probably familiar with *The Life and Times of Jesus the Messiah*. But he had also read another one of Edersheim's books, *The Temple: Its Ministry and Services,* illustrating the fact that at least this additional volume of Edersheim's had made its way to Utah. Elder Smith cited the following reference in a general conference talk in April 1936 on the centennial anniversary of the Prophet Joseph Smith receiving the keys of this dispensation from Moses, Elias, and Elijah in the Kirtland Temple.

## ELIJAH'S PASSOVER RETURN

One hundred years earlier on April 3, 1836, a church meeting had been held in the Kirtland Temple. After officiating and partaking of the sacrament, the Prophet Joseph Smith and Oliver Cowdery retired to the pulpit, having the veils of the temple dropped to separate them from others. They both knelt in prayer. After rising from their prayer, a vision opened up to both of them:

The veil was taken from our minds and the eyes of our understanding were opened.

We saw the Lord standing upon the breastwork of the pulpit, before us. . . .

And his voice was as the sound of the rushing of great waters, even the voice of Jehovah, saying:

I am the first and the last; I am he who liveth, I am he would was slain; I am your advocate with the Father. . . .

For behold, I have accepted this house, and my name shall be here; and I will manifest myself to my people in mercy in this house. . . .

After this vision closed, the heavens were again opened unto us; and Moses appeared before us, and committed unto us the keys of the gathering of Israel. . . .

After this, Elias appeared, and committed the dispensation of the gospel of Abraham. . . .

After this vision had closed, another great and glorious vision burst upon us; for Elijah the prophet, who was taken to heaven without tasting death, stood before us, and said:

Behold the time has fully come. . . .

To turn the hearts of the fathers to the children, and the children to the fathers, lest the whole earth be smitten with a curse—

Therefore, the keys of this dispensation are committed into your hands; and by this ye may know that the great and dreadful day of the Lord is near, even at the doors. (D&C 110:1–4, 7–8, 11–16)

"IN INSTITUTING HIS OWN Supper, the Lord Jesus connected the symbol, not of judgment, but of his dying love, with his third cup."
—Alfred Edersheim

One hundred years later, Elder Joseph Fielding Smith pointed out that this had happened at the same time that Jews all around the world were celebrating the Passover. During the Paschal service, Jewish families would have left a door open to admit Elijah's entrance. Elder Smith used Edersheim's explanation of this sacred Jewish tradition when he said, "I want to call your attention to an incident which I think is of some importance. I am going to read to you a statement from Alfred Edersheim in his work *The Temple*. Speaking of the Paschal Feast and the Lord's Supper, he says:

> Jewish tradition has this curious conceit: that the most important events in Israel's history were connected with the Paschal season. . . . And so also in the last days it would be the Paschal night when the final judgment should come upon Edom and the glorious deliverance of Israel take place. Hence to this day, in every Jewish home, at a certain part of the Paschal service—just after the "third cup," or the "cup of blessing," has been drunk—the door is opened to admit Elijah the prophet as forerunner of the Messiah, while appropriate passages are at the same time read which foretell the destruction of all heathen nations. It is a remarkable coincidence that, in instituting his own Supper, the Lord Jesus connected the symbol, not of judgment, but of his dying love, with his third cup.[1]

"It was, I am informed, on the third day of April, 1836, that the Jews, in their homes at the Paschal feast, opened their doors for Elijah to enter. On that very day, Elijah did enter,"[2] concluded Joseph Fielding Smith.

Later, as president of the Church, Smith cited this same passage in his book *Restoration of All Things*[3] and included this quote in the 1949 Melchizedek Priesthood Course of Study, *Church History and Modern Revelation*.[4] Daniel Ludlow has also cited President Smith quoting Edersheim on this identical point of doctrine in both *A Companion to Your Study of the Doctrine and Covenants*[5] and *A Companion to Your Study of the Old Testament*.[6]

## OTHER SIGNIFICANT REFERENCES

President Smith is not the only one to quote Edersheim in a general conference talk. Elder William J. Critchlow Jr. quoted him in general conference on October 1966.[7] Elder Critchlow used Edersheim as an authority on Jewish traditions during the time of Christ and cited from *The Life and Times of Jesus the Messiah*: " 'The Jewish Talmud makes it plain that baptism,' a gospel ordinance, 'was required for admission to the Church,' "[8] connecting the Old Testament ordinance of baptism with the New Testament and the restored covenant of baptism.

Perhaps President Smith's use of Edersheim paved the way for his son-in-law, Elder Bruce R. McConkie, to reference Edersheim so extensively in his writings about the Savior. The name of Alfred Edersheim had then been heard by the Church at large. He had testified that the Savior connected the symbol of the Passover and the sacrament with his love, not with his judgment. Joseph Smith and Oliver Cowdery had partaken of the sacrament as the Jews were partaking of the Passover meal. This remembrance of his sacrifice lifted the veil and brought the keys of his kingdom back to the earth, bringing "the promise of the bright Day at His Coming." [9]

## NOTES

1. Edersheim, *Temple*, 180–81.
2. Joseph Fielding Smith, CR, Apr. 1936, 74–75.
3. Smith, *The Restoration of All Things*, 170.
4. Smith, *Church History and Modern Revelation*, 84.
5. Ludlow, *A Companion to Your Study of the Doctrine and Covenants*, 1:568.
6. Ludlow, *A Companion to Your Study of the Old Testament*, 57–58.
7. William J. Critchlow Jr., CR, Oct. 1966, 30–31.
8. Edersheim, *Jesus the Messiah*, 745 (2:395).
9. Edersheim, *Jesus the Messiah*, 827–28 (2:512–13).

# CHAPTER FIFTEEN

# BRUCE R. MCCONKIE:
# EDERSHEIM, OUR LEARNED FRIEND

IN THE 1960s, BRUCE R. McConkie referred to Edersheim in his three-volume work *Doctrinal New Testament Commentary*. Though he quoted Edersheim three times and referred to an opinion of his once in that work, he appears not to have had his own copy of *The Life and Times of Jesus the Messiah*, since all his quotes are cited as coming from Talmage's *Jesus the Christ*.[1] However, by the time McConkie wrote his four-volume work *The Mortal Messiah* (published 1979–81), he had clearly "found" Alfred Edersheim. In these volumes he quoted Edersheim at length more than 120 times—one quote several pages long—from the three prominent works of Edersheim: *The Life and Times of Jesus the Messiah*, *Sketches of Jewish Social Life*, and *The Temple: Its Ministry and Services*.[2]

## OUR LEARNED FRIEND

Bruce R. McConkie showed a tremendous respect and love for Alfred Edersheim. Toward the end of Elder McConkie's multi-volume work *The Mortal Messiah*, he draws "on our learned friend, Edersheim"[3] for an enlightening and remarkable coincidence about the hall the Savior requested for his last Passover meal. The Savior asked Peter and

John to prepare for the Paschal feast. In Edersheim's translation of the Savior's instructions, he felt a better translation of the original words written in Luke 22:11 and Mark 14:14 would have been "Where is my hostelry [or hall], where I shall eat the Passover with My disciples?"[4] Initially, the Apostles had asked the good man of the house for the hall, or *katalyma*, which would have been downstairs overlooking the stables and animals, not the guestchamber upstairs. Edersheim explained:

> The Master would only ask for "the hall": as He was born in a Katalyma, so He would have been content to eat there His last Meal—at the same time meal, feast, sacrifice, and institution. But the unnamed disciple would assign to Him, not the Hall, but the best and chiefest, "the upper chamber," or Aliyah, at the same time the most honourable and the most retired place, where from the outside stairs entrance and departure might be had without passing through the house.[5]

Elder McConkie discussed this passage: "He who was born in a hostelry—Katalyma—was content to ask for His last meal in a Katalyma. Born in the humblest of circumstances, he was prepared to remain in them all his days. . . . But as we have seen—and as Jesus foreknew—the Goodman of the house took Peter and John to 'a large upper room.' " As Mark explained, "And he will shew you a large upper room furnished and prepared: there make ready for us" (Mark 14:15).

## AN ALIYAH IS AN UPPER ROOM
which is considered the most honorable and
private place in the home.

McConkie used other commentators and writers on the life of Jesus Christ to write his series of books on the Savior's life and his eternal mission. Frederick W. Farrar's *Life of Christ* (1874) and Dummelow's *A Commentary on the Holy Bible* (1908) are two books McConkie cited a great deal, along with Edersheim's works. All of these books were used in McConkie's description of the Lord's Last Supper; yet, in comparing

Edersheim, Farrar, and Dummelow's commentary on the Savior's institution of the sacrament, McConkie said, "Edersheim may be taken as
the most authoritative in cases where views are divergent."[6]

## JEWISH SABBATH TRADITIONS

McConkie uses Edersheim extensively when describing Jewish
traditions such as Sabbath day practices, temple worship, and family
life, and to describe Jewish symbols and his witness of Jesus Christ as
the Messiah. While discussing the Feast of Tabernacles, McConkie
acknowledges taking his "cues and quotations from Edersheim (*Temple*,
pp. 268–87), but tempering his views with the added light and knowledge revealed in the dispensation of the fulness of times."[7]

In the chapter "Jewish Sabbaths in Jesus' Day," McConkie quotes
Edersheim eight times in five pages to illustrate the ridiculous and
tedious nature of Sabbath day observance for Jews. On the Sabbath,
Jehovah commanded that "thou shalt not do any work, thou, nor
thy son, nor thy daughter, thy manservant, nor thy maidservant, nor
thy cattle, nor thy stranger that is within thy gates" (Exodus 20:10).
The practical problem for the Jews became defining what work was.
Through the generations, the definition of what could or could not be
done on the Sabbath had become more and more tedious. The Jewish
law in Jesus' day had categorized thirty-nine principle types of work
forbidden on the Sabbath. Defining what constituted these types of
work required detailed explanations and illustrations. For example,
Edersheim enumerates,

> Distinctions like the following are made: "A radish may be
> dipped into sale, but not left in it too long, since this would be to
> make a pickle. A new dress might be put on, irrespective of the
> danger that in so doing it might be torn. Mud on the dress might be
> crushed in the hand and shaken off, but the dress must not be rubbed
> (for fear of affecting the material). If a person took a bath, opinions
> are divided, whether the whole body should be dried at once, or limb
> after limb."[8]

In Jeremiah 17:21–22, the Lord said, "Take heed to yourselves,
and bear no burden on the sabbath day, nor bring it in by the gates
of Jerusalem; Neither carry forth a burden out of your houses on the
sabbath day, neither do ye any work, but hallow ye the sabbath day,

as I commanded your fathers." This became another matter of long and tedious definitions of what constituted a burden. Anything that could be put to a practical use, no matter how trifling, was considered a burden: "Thus two horse's hairs might be made into a birdtrap; a scrap of clean paper into a custom-house notice; a small piece of paper written upon might be converted into a wrapper for a small flagon. In all these cases, therefore, transport would involve sin."[9]

If your house caught fire on the Sabbath, one could not put out the fire and save the building, for that was clearly work. But the scriptures and phylacteries and food and drink needed for the Sabbath might be rescued.

The Savior's healing was considered work because the "practice of the healing arts was work and therefore could not be done on the Sabbath. Broken bones could not be set; surgical operations were not allowed; emetics could not be given. 'A plaster might be worn, provided its object was to prevent the wound from getting worse, not to heal it, for that would have been work.' "[10]

The Jews had also come up with practical ways to get around some of these restrictions. For example, a man could place a beam, a wire, or a rope across an alley or a narrow street, making all the houses thereon one dwelling "so that everything was lawful there which a man might do on the Sabbath in his own house."[11] On Friday before the Sabbath, a man could deposit food for two meals at a distance of two thousand cubits (the distance of one day's journey). That place then became his dwelling as well and he could carry burdens an extra two thousand cubits. These are just a small sampling of the system of Sabbath observance in place during Jesus' time.

McConkie clarifies his use of Edersheim and another writer, Cunningham Geikie, in trying to make clear the many Jewish laws and regulations surrounding the Sabbath day: "These comments about Jewish Sabbath observance and the illustrations set forth are digested from Edersheim, pages 775–87, and from Geikie, pages 448–50, both of which authors, in turn, digested their material from the Mishnah."[12] These writers had read and studied the many pages of detailed laws and Sabbath regulations in the Mishnah and gave a much shorter explanation of these Jewish traditions. In comparison to the twelve pages in Edersheim's *Life and Times of Jesus the Messiah*, the Mishnah contains thirty-seven pages detailing the Sabbath day regulations of ancient Jews.

## JEWISH THEOLOGICAL VIEWS

When the Savior was teaching his disciples about who was the greatest in the kingdom of heaven, he gathered a small child in his arms and said, "Whosoever shall receive one of such children in my name, receiveth me: and whosoever shall receive me, receiveth not me, but him that sent me" (Mark 9:37). He then taught them not to offend these little ones, for offenses will come. Every one of them would experience trials and they would have to stand firm in their testimony of him. He warned them, "For every one shall be salted with fire, and every sacrifice shall be salted with salt. Salt is good: but if the salt have lost his saltness, wherewith will ye season it? Have salt in yourselves, and have peace one with another" (Mark 9:49–50).

Edersheim explains this passage about salt, fire, and sacrifices:

> It is a well-known law, that every sacrifice burned on the Altar must be salted with salt. Indeed, according to the Talmud, not only every such offering, but even the wood with which the sacrificial fire was kindled, was sprinkled with salt. Salt symbolized to the Jews of that time the incorruptible and the higher. Thus, the soul was compared to the salt and it was said concerning the dead: "Shake off the salt, and throw the flesh to the dogs." The Bible was compared to salt; so was acuteness of intellect. Lastly, the question: "if the salt have lost its savour, wherewith will ye season it?" Seems to have been proverbial, and occurs in exactly the same words in the Talmud.[13]

## THE ALTAR WAS A "SQUARE OF

not less than 48 feet. . . . Close by was the great heap of salt, from which every sacrifice must be salted with salt."—Alfred Edersheim

The only way salt can be corrupted is by mixing it with dirt and filth. This will take away its purity. If we have lost our savor, then we have become corrupted by the world and are of no use spiritually. Edersheim continued,

If ye yourselves are not purified and clean; if ye have not risen above worldly things, including your bickerings about greatness; if ye have lost the spirit of the gospel, how shall your spiritual sacrifices be purified? "Hence, have salt in yourselves," but do not let that salt be corrupted by making it an occasion of offence to others, or among yourselves, as in the dispute by the way, or in the disposition of mind that led to it, or in forbidding others to work who follow not with you, but "be at peace among yourselves."[14]

After his discussion on salt, sacrifices, and tribulation by fire, McConkie discusses the Savior's comment: "Take heed that ye despise not one of these little ones; for I say unto you, That in heaven their angels do always behold the face of my Father which is in heaven" (Matthew 18:10). McConkie states that in order to understand this pronouncement, "we yet again must turn to the Jewish theological context in which it was made."[15] Then, McConkie quotes Edersheim for clarification: "In the Jewish view, only the chiefest of the Angels were before the face of God within the curtained Veil, or Pargod, while the others, ranged in different classes, stood outside and awaited his behest. The distinction which the former enjoyed was always to behold His Face, and to hear and know directly the Divine counsels and commands."[16]

The Savior's reference to "their angels do always behold the face of my Father" was refuting the disciples' Jewish concept of the hierarchy of the angelic world. Instead of the great angels of Michael, Raphael, and Gabriel standing in God's presence, the Savior clarified that these angels of little children also beheld the face of "my Father." His words "my Father" also renewed his witness of divine Sonship. McConkie also points out that this entire statement "was an allusion to preexistence; perhaps it was an outright teaching of that doctrine, for the words recorded may be only a small part of what Jesus then said. Truly, the spirits of all children, prior to entering the moral body, dwell in the presence of the Father. They see his face, hear his voice, and know his teachings."[17]

In McConkie's view, Edersheim's writings are an authoritative resource for Jewish theological traditions. Even though Edersheim did not have the further light and knowledge of the restored gospel of Jesus Christ, his explanations of Jewish theological traditions shed greater light and understanding of Jesus' words and testimony of his divine mission here upon the earth.

## DISAGREEING WITH EDERSHEIM

Similar to B. H. Roberts, Elder McConkie did not always agree with Edersheim. There was one point on which McConkie strongly disagreed with Edersheim: "Edersheim argues—falsely, we are confident to assert—that Jesus was never formally tried by the Sanhedrin." Edersheim does give an instructive presentation describing the illegalities of the night's proceedings had it really been a trial. Talmage and other biblical scholars, including McConkie, believe that the events in Caiaphas's palace were a formal trial. Edersheim contends, "It is admitted on all hands, that forty years before the destruction of the Temple the Sanhedrin ceased to pronounce capital sentences. This alone would be sufficient. But besides, the trial and sentence of Jesus in the Palace of Caiaphas would (as already stated) have outraged every principle of Jewish criminal law and procedure." Edersheim continues to enumerate all the reasons the Sanhedrin could not have tried and sentenced the Savior. Elder McConkie refutes Edersheim's claims with the retort: "And so it did!"[18]

That does not mean that Edersheim does not place the blame for the condemnation and death of the Savior on the Sanhedrists. He wrote, "But although Christ was not tried and sentenced in a formal meeting of the Sanhedrin, there can alas! be no question that His Condemnation and Death were the work, if not of the Sanhedrin, yet of the Sanhedrists." In spite of McConkie's disagreement with Edersheim, he still cites several paragraphs from Edersheim's work on the topic, letting Edersheim speak for himself to show both sides of the argument.[19]

## EDERSHEIM—A LITERARY GEM

Elder McConkie offered an opinion about modern sectarian commentaries and biographies on Christ judging most of them as "far from faith promoting." Instead, he felt "it is necessary to go back a hundred years or so to find authors who believed in the divine Sonship with sufficient fervor to accept the New Testament passages as meaning what they say."[20]

Edersheim's works and other nearly century-old commentaries are cited extensively in *The Mortal Messiah*. As an explanation, Elder McConkie stated:

I have not hesitated to quote selected literary gems and to paraphrase others, as is also the case, occasionally, throughout this work,
with particular reference to the writings of Edersheim and Farrar,
two of the best sectarian authors. Short of receiving personal revelation on all points, no one author can think of all the meanings or set
forth every nuance of thought on all points. Further, it seems a waste
of literary talent not to preserve some of the thoughts and modes of
expression that those of old, who wrote on the same subjects, were
led by the spirit of truth to record.[21]

Edersheim devoted seven years of thoughtful, spiritual labor and
research to write *The Life and Times of Jesus the Messiah*. He finished
his work on Easter morning in 1883. Similarly, Elder McConkie took
many years to finish his epic work *The Mortal Messiah*, and he finished it in 1981, nearly one hundred years after Edersheim's death.
Acknowledging their similarities, McConkie quoted Edersheim's
words at the end of his own writings on the life of Jesus Christ:

Our task is ended—and we also worship and look up. And we
go back from this sight into a hostile world, to love, and to live, and
to work for the Risen Christ. But as earth's day is growing dim,
and, with earth's gathering darkness, breaks over it heaven's storm,
we ring out—as of old they were wont, from church-tower, to the
mariners that hugged a rock-bound coast—our Easter-bells to guide
them who are belated, over the storm-tossed sea, beyond the offerings, all ye people; worship in faith, for—"This Jesus, Which was
received up for you into heaven, shall so come, in like manner as ye
beheld Him going into Heaven."[22]

# NOTES

1. McConkie, *Doctrinal New Testament Commentary*, 1:783–84, 788, 810,
   816.
2. McConkie, *The Mortal Messiah*, 1:43, 49, 91, 112–14, 122–23, 126–27,
   130–40, 157, 164, 168, 171–77, 180, 184–86, 191, 193, 207–12, 218–
   19, 225–27, 239–40, 247, 249–51, 272, 279–80, 288, 334–35, 359, 363,
   397–98, 449, 460, 467, 470–71, 490, 494–95, 504–5. *The Mortal Messiah*,
   *Book 2*, 10, 28, 63, 65, 87, 89–90 113, 126, 129, 184–85, 199, 202–3,
   207, 211–12, 228, 242–43, 261, 268–69, 277, 281–82, 302, 339, 349,
   364, 368, 373–74, 385–89. *The Mortal Messiah, Book 3*, 16, 20, 24–25, 30,
   40–42, 69, 80, 87–88, 96, 103, 123, 134–36, 145, 148, 165, 170, 175–76,

178, 184, 195–97, 205, 246, 253, 320, 322, 353–54, 370–71, 393, 466, 476. *The Mortal Messiah, Book 4*, 6–7, 14–15, 18, 20, 28, 30, 40–41, 46, 67, 92–93, 122, 124, 130, 148, 152, 155–57, 163, 181, 198–203, 215, 229–30, 235, 238–39, 248, 261, 270, 285, 425.

3. McConkie, *The Mortal Messiah*, 4:22.
4. Edersheim, *Jesus the Messiah*, 807 (2:483). Compare Luke 22:10–11 and Mark 14:14.
5. Edersheim, *Jesus the Messiah*, 808 (2:484).
6. McConkie, *The Mortal Messiah*, 4:66, footnote 6.
7. McConkie, *The Mortal Messiah*, 1:171.
8. McConkie, *The Mortal Messiah*, 1:207; Edersheim, *Jesus the Messiah*, 1051 (2:783).
9. McConkie, *The Mortal Messiah*, 1:208; Edersheim, *Jesus the Messiah*, 1052 (2:784).
10. McConkie, *The Mortal Messiah*, 1:210.
11. McConkie, *The Mortal Messiah*, 1:209.
12. McConkie, *The Mortal Messiah*, 1:212, footnote 1.
13. McConkie, *The Mortal Messiah*, 3:88, note 2; Edersheim, *Jesus the Messiah*, 557–58 (2:121–22).
14. McConkie, *The Mortal Messiah*, 3:87; Edersheim, *Jesus the Messiah*, 557 (2:121).
15. McConkie, *The Mortal Messiah*, 3:87.
16. Edersheim, *Jesus the Messiah*, 558 (2:122).
17. McConkie, *The Mortal Messiah*, 3:88.
18. McConkie, *The Mortal Messiah*, 4:169, read the entire note 3; Edersheim, *Jesus the Messiah*, 857–59 (2:556–58).
19. McConkie, *The Mortal Messiah*, 4:169.
20. McConkie, *The Mortal Messiah*, 4:425, footnote 2.
21. McConkie, *The Mortal Messiah*, 2:338, footnote 2.
22. McConkie, *The Mortal Messiah*, 4:425, footnote 3; Edersheim, *Jesus the Messiah*, 921–22 (2:652).

# CHAPTER SIXTEEN

# EDERSHEIM TODAY

WITH ELDER MCCONKIE'S EXTENDED quotations and clear blessing, Edersheim citations have become very common in the Latter-day Saint publishing community. Quotations from Edersheim's works can be found in modern LDS books by Joseph Fielding McConkie, Gerald Lund, Roy Doxey, Daniel Ludlow, Richard Draper, Milton Backman, Robert Millet, and even the *Church News*. Often, contemporary LDS authors reference Edersheim indirectly by quoting earlier Church leaders who are quoting Edersheim. Other references are new Edersheim quotations not referenced previously by others, illustrating the fact that he is still being read.

## JOSEPH FIELDING MCCONKIE

Joseph Fielding McConkie's book *Gospel Symbolism* (1999) is a good example of the way Edersheim is being referenced by current LDS authors. He quoted his father, Elder Bruce R. McConkie, quoting Edersheim about the symbolism of the scapegoat: "By lot one of the goats was to be designated as the goat of the Lord, the name Jehovah being placed upon him."[1] Yet, in a discussion of the Sabbath, McConkie quotes Edersheim directly: "Edersheim observes that 'the

Sabbath was symbolic of the millennial kingdom at the end of the six thousand years' dispensation, when the Lord would reign over all, and His glory and service fill the earth with thanksgiving.' "[2]

Joseph Fielding McConkie uses Edersheim quotes for many of the same reasons earlier authors did, focusing on his expertise in Jewish customs, the Jewish way of life, and temple worship. Additionally, he referenced Edersheim's book *Bible History: Old Testament*, using Edersheim's insights about the Old Testament, rather than just his New Testament knowledge. For example, McConkie pointed out that Edersheim was aware that Joseph's coat of many colors was really a symbol of his birthright and priesthood. He quoted Edersheim, who wrote, "But in truth it was not a 'coat of many colours,' but a tunic reaching down the arms and feet such as princes and persons of distinction wore, and it betokened to Joseph's brothers only too clearly, their father intended to transfer to Joseph the right of the first born."[3]

McConkie used the symbol of Joseph's dead body, pointing the children toward their covenant responsibilities in the land of promise and away from the world, as represented by Egypt. When leaving Egypt, Moses and the children of Israel took the coffin of Joseph with them. Before his death, Joseph had made the children of Israel promise to takes his bones with them. Edersheim saw the symbol of Joseph's dead body as speaking to Israel and telling them that they were only temporary visitors in Egypt. Their real home was back in the land of the Lord's promise and covenant. Edersheim wrote:

> In obedience to his wishes they embalmed his body, and laid it in one of those Egyptian coffins, generally made of sycamore wood, which resembled the shape of the human body. And there, through ages of suffering and bondage, stood the figure—like coffin of Joseph, ready to be lifted and carried thence when the sure hour of deliverance had come. Thus Joseph, being dead, yet spake to Israel, telling them that they were only temporary sojourners in Egypt, that their eyes must be turned away from Egypt unto the land of promise, and that in the patience of faith they must wait for that hour when God would certainly and graciously fulfill His own promises.[4]

McConkie discussed the symbolism of Moses striking a rock and water flowing from it. In this Old Testament event, he saw that Edersheim understood the New Testament significance of the Living Waters flowing from the rock of our Redeemer: "Edersheim writes,

'And from the river side of the parched rock living waters flowed,' suggesting to our minds the image of Christ upon the cross, his side pierced with a Roman spear giving forth blood and water that all might live (John 19:34)."[5] Edersheim recognized that the symbolism of the Old Testament pointed to the future fulfillment of prophecy in the earthly life and mission of the Savior.

## OTHER CURRENT LDS WRITERS

In comparing the dispensations of the Old and New Testaments, Camille Fronk cited Edersheim's description of baptism for Jews living the Old Testament law. The act of baptism was performed for those desiring admission or readmission into Judaism. Referring to Talmudic writings, Edersheim wrote, "The baptism was to be performed in the presence of three witnesses. . . . The person to be baptized, having cut his hair and nails, undressed completely, made fresh profession of his faith, before what were designated 'the fathers of the baptism' and then immersed completely, so that every part of the body was touched by the water. The rite would, of course, be accompanied by exhortations and benedictions."[6]

Edersheim described the purpose and desired outcome of this baptism as becoming a new man or a little child, born anew: "As he stepped out of these waters he was considered as 'born anew'—the language of the Rabbis, as if he were 'a little child just born' as 'a child of one day.' . . . More especially was he to regard himself as a new man in reference to his past. Country, home, habits, friends, and relations were all changed. The past, with all that had belonged to it, was past, and he was a new man—the old, with its defilements, was buried in the waters of baptism."[7]

Fronk remarked that Edersheim's comments "on Jewish tradition symbolize being 'born again' and becoming a new creature with verbal commitments and total immersion in water."[8] These Old Testament traditions had their realization in Jesus Christ as he instituted the new covenant of baptism.

Edersheim's explanations of Jewish traditions and rites have been used by many other LDS contemporary authors. Here are a few examples:

- Donald W. and Jay A. Parry reference Edersheim's discussion of the scapegoat in their book *Understanding the Signs of the Times*.[9]

- D. Kelly Ogden reference Edersheim's commentary on Jesus' announcement that he was the Light of the World (John 8:12) in the *Church News*.[10]
- R. Scott Lloyd quotes Edersheim pointing out that all scriptures direct us to Christ, including the Old Testament, also in the *Church News*.[11]
- Joseph Fielding McConkie and Robert L. Millet refer to Edersheim's description of the first fruits of Christ in *Doctrinal Commentary on the Book of Mormon*.[12]
- Gerald N. Lund quotes an ancient rabbinical saying found in Edersheim's works about Judea and Galilee in *A Celebration of Christmas*.[13]
- Milton V. Backman and Robert L. Millet quote Edersheim's description of Elijah's coming during the Passover in *Studies in Scripture, Vol. 1: The Doctrine and Covenants*.[14]
- George A. Horton Jr. cites another rabbinical saying referred to by Edersheim about the temple as the center of worship in *The Pearl of Great Price: Revelations from God*.[15]
- William B. Smart quotes a beautiful single line of Edersheim's writing in *Messages for a Happier Life*: "While He lay in prayer, they lay in sleep; and yet where soul-agony leads not to the one, it often induces the other."[16]

## IS EDERSHEIM RELEVANT FOR US TODAY?

Obviously, Edersheim is still being referenced today. The question is, should he be? In order to answer this question, I solicited the opinions of biblical scholars inside and outside of the LDS Church community. Dr. David Spriggs, a Bible and Church consultant for the Bible Society in Coventry, England,[17] knew Edersheim only peripherally. Even though Edersheim was an Anglican minister of some renown over 130 years ago, Spriggs felt Edersheim would be dismissed because his writings do not take into account the archaeological and philological material of the last hundred years. In a cyclic way, Spriggs speculated that if religion professors do not require their students to read Edersheim, then students would not read or buy his books. He believed because Edersheim is not included as part of their religious curriculum, they will not take the opportunity to gain from his insights.

Spriggs generalized that modern biblical scholars "have an attitude which is rather dismissive of anything that is not 'up to date.'" Spriggs also felt Edersheim's nineteenth century writing style was "indirect and long-winded," and the "lack of colour pictures and diagrams to attract and keep attention" may be difficult to handle for the general reader.

This mirrors a comment made by Dr. John W. Welch, editor of *BYU Studies*, in reference to Edersheim's writings about the Septuagint: "With the discovery of the Dead Sea Scrolls, it is apparent that the transmission of the LXX is much more complex than had been supposed."[18] Certainly, modern discoveries and easier access to source documents enable current gospel scholars to delve more deeply into text-related issues than Edersheim and other scholars of his day could possibly achieve. This is true not only of Edersheim's writings about the Septuagint, but of other scriptural analyses he makes in his gospel commentaries. Yet all scriptural writers who were contemporaries of Edersheim were under this same pall of ignorance. That does not mean all of their works should be summarily discarded.

Dr. Eugene J. Mayhew, professor of Old Testament history at Michigan Theological Seminary (MTS) felt differently than Dr. Spriggs. He finds many benefits from Edersheim's *Life and Times of Jesus the Messiah*, even when compared with later works, because of the "many Jewish insights that are often neglected or overlooked in other books."[19] Mayhew said, "Edersheim is still used here at MTS along with many other works—past and present." Mayhew does not see himself as an Edersheim "groupie," but he still appreciates Edersheim's works and insights.

Elder Ted E. Brewerton, an emeritus member of the First Quorum of the Seventy, is working with a group of LDS translators to create the LDS Church edition of the Spanish Bible. He mentioned that two of Edersheim's texts, *The Temple* and *The Life and Times of Jesus the Messiah*, have been used as references. These books have given "details regarding the Law of Moses, e.g. sacrifices, Joseph's coat of many colors, etc. It enlarges our understanding, even though we do not quote him in our Bible text."[20]

Edersheim's own scholarship and study should be highlighted and not disparaged. He described his learning as embodying "the results of many years' study, in which I have availed myself of every help within my reach. It might seem affectation if I were to enumerate the names of all the authorities consulted or books read in the course of these studies."[21]

Even though Edersheim's books are not usually incorporated in biblical studies curricula, his books still continue to be read. People from a variety of faiths find his books appealing in spite of his nineteenth century writing style and lack of illustrations. There are, however, new copies of his books being published today with color photos, tables, and diagrams for those who need the addition of pictorial presentations.[22]

From an LDS historical perspective, Edersheim's writings have been inextricably mixed with our writings. It is important to acknowledge his work and his influence on LDS authors and General Authorities. Edersheim's view of Jewish prophecy fulfilled in Christ has placed an indelible mark on LDS thought.

## THE REAL REASON FOR READING EDERSHEIM— HIS TESTIMONY OF THE SAVIOR

There is a power in Edersheim's testimony of Jesus Christ that transcends the need for current source documentation. Edersheim realized the symbolic representation of the Lord in all things. He saw Jesus in the rituals at the temple, the observance of the Sabbath, the ritual clothing, the first fruits of the field, and the words of the Old Testament. From the time of Adam, the Lord has taught his children, "And behold, all things have their likeness, and all things are created and made to bear record of me, both things which are temporal, and things which are spiritual; things which are in the heavens above, and things which are on the earth, and things which are in the earth, and things which are under the earth, both above and beneath: all things bear record of me" (Moses 6:63).

"ALL I REALLY KNOW OF GOD
—all I want to know of God—is in Christ. My god is only God in Christ; I know no other, and I do not want to know any other than as there revealed."—Alfred Edersheim

Edersheim recognized the Lord Jesus Christ the moment he read the Sermon on the Mount. He was able to hear his words and become a new man. Edersheim tried to give his best and most earnest labor "to write what I believed to be true, irrespective of party or received opinions."[23] He considered his writing a sacred duty and dedicated his writing to the Lord while bearing a fervent testimony of Jesus Christ throughout. He wrote, "My deepest and most earnest prayer is that He, in Whose Service I have desired to write these book[s], would graciously accept the humble service—forgive what is mistaken and bless what is true."[24]

He felt a great kinship with New Testament prophets who also had to change their way of thinking. They, too, were Jews that had come to accept Jesus Christ as their Messiah. He was their Messiah-king the prophets had foretold would come. His humble life was the fulfillment of thousands of years of prophecy.

Peter asked the question that Edersheim understood deep in his heart: "Lord, to whom shall we go?" Peter's answer was Edersheim's answer, as shown by his life: "Thou has the words of eternal life. And we believe and are sure that thou art that Christ, the son of the living God" (John 6:68–69). His testimony was firm according to the best light and knowledge he had. His words showed intimations of a "greater light" as he was an Elias of a "greater day."[25]

I have the same prayer in my heart, as did Elder Bruce R. McConkie, that the fact that he did not hear the restored gospel of Jesus Christ during his earthly life has been rectified, perhaps by the very men who benefited from his writings. It is my hope that he has received the added light and knowledge of the fulness of the gospel of Jesus Christ[26] and that he continues to pursue "that strait and narrow course that will make [him] an inheritor of the fulness of our Father's kingdom."[27]

## NOTES

1. McConkie, *Gospel Symbolism*, 83.
2. McConkie, *Gospel Symbolism*, 199.
3. McConkie, *Gospel Symbolism*, 31; Edersheim, *Bible History*, 1:144.
4. McConkie, *Gospel Symbolism*, 56; Edersheim, *Bible History*, 1:189–90.
5. McConkie, *Gospel Symbolism*, 56; Edersheim, *Bible History*, 2:101.
6. Fronk, "The Everlasting Gospel: A Comparison of Dispensations,"

184–185; Edersheim, *Jesus the Messiah*, 1014–16 (2:745–47), Appendix 12. See also Edersheim's discussion of "Baptism of Repentance," 186–90 (1:270–74).

7. Fronk, "The Everlasting Gospel: A Comparison of Dispensations," 184.

8. Fronk, "The Everlasting Gospel: A Comparison of Dispensations," 185.

9. Parry and Parry, *Understanding the Signs of the Times*, 289.

10. D. Kelly Ogden, *Church News*, 7 Jan. 1995.

11. R. Scott Lloyd, *Church News*, 6 Jan. 1990.

12. McConkie and Millet, *Doctrinal Commentary on the Book of Mormon*, 2:42.

13. Lund, *A Celebration of Christmas*, 30.

14. Backman and Millet, "Heavenly Manifestations in the Kirtland Temple," 426–27.

15. Horton, *The Pearl of Great Price: Revelations from God*, 199.

16. Smart, *Messages for a Happier Life: Inspiring Essays from the Church News*, 19.

17. The quotes in this paragraph come from an email dated 22 June 2006 and are used by permission of Dr. Spriggs.

18. Roberts, *The Truth, the Way, the Life*, 173, footnote 1.

19. The quotes in this paragraph come from an email dated 8 Aug. 2006 and are used by permission of Dr. Mayhew.

20. The quotes in this paragraph come from an email dated 29 June 2006 and are used by permission of Elder Brewerton.

21. Edersheim, *Sketches*, viii.

22. Edersheim, *The Temple: Its Ministry and Services* (Grand Rapids, MI: Kregel Publications, 1997).

23. Edersheim, *Jesus the Messiah*, xvi.

24. Edersheim, *Jesus the Messiah*, xvi. This is at the end of his preface for the first edition of *The Life and Times of Jesus the Messiah*.

25. McConkie, *The Mortal Messiah*, 4:180, footnote 1.

26. According to the IGI, Alfred Edersheim's temple work has already been done.

27. McConkie, *The Mortal Messiah*, 4:180, footnote 1.

# APPENDIX

Table 1: Major publications of Alfred Edersheim[1]

| DATE | PUBLICATION TITLE | DESCRIPTION |
|---|---|---|
| 1842 | *Heinrich* | A story published while Edersheim was a student at the University of Pesth, Hungary. He published other stories during this time. |
| 1847 | *The Jubilee Rhythm of St. Bernard of Clairvaux on the Name of Jesus and Other Hymns* | A collection of hymns, mostly Latin songs, translated by Edersheim (London: James Nisbet & Co.). |
| 1851 | *Whose Is Thine Heart* | Published in London. |
| 1854 | *Historical Development of Speculative Philosophy from 1854: Kant to Hegel* | Book by Heinrich Moritz Chalybaeus translated from German by Edersheim (Edinburgh: T & T Clark). |
| 1856 | *History of the Jewish Nation after the Destruction of Jerusalem by Titus* | Historical work published in Edinburgh. |

| DATE | PUBLICATION TITLE | DESCRIPTION |
| --- | --- | --- |
| 1857 | *The History of Israel and Judah from the Decline of the Two Kingdoms to the Assyrian and Babylonian Captivity* | Historical work (New York: James Pott & Company). |
| 1858 | *Bohemian Reformers and German Politicians: A Contribution to the History of Protestantism* | Essays by Edersheim and W. Hanna. |
| 1859 | *History of the Old Covenant* | Book by Dr. Johann Heinrich Durtz translated from German by Edersheim (Edinburgh: T & T Clark). |
| 1859 | *Commentary on St. Mather* | Book by John Peter Lange translated from German by Edersheim (Edinburgh: T & T Clark). |
| 1860 | *History of the Christian Church to the Reformation* | Book by Johann Heinrich Kurtz translated from German by Edersheim. |
| 1866 | *The Golden Diary of the Heart: Converse with Jesus in the Book of Psalms* | A devotional book published in London. |
| 1869 | *Elisha the Prophet: His Life and Times* | A series of lectures published in London and republished under the title *Elisha the Prophet, A Type of Christ* (1873). |
| 1871 | *Robbie and His Mother* | Published by Religious Tract Society in London. |
| 1872 | *True to the End* | Published in London. |
| 1872 | *Miriam Rosenbaum: A Story of Jewish Life* | Published in London. |
| 1874 | *The Temple: Its Ministry and Services at the Time of Jesus Christ* | Published by Religious Tract Society in London. Still in print. |
| 1875–1887 | *Bible History* | A seven-volume series covering the history of the Old Testament from Genesis to Jeremiah. Still in print. |

| DATE | PUBLICATION TITLE | DESCRIPTION |
|------|-------------------|-------------|
| 1876 | *The Exodus and the Wanderings in the Wilderness* | Published by Revell. |
| 1876 | *Sketches of Jewish Social Life in the Days of Christ* | Still in print. |
| 1877 | *Israel in Canaan Under Joshua and Judges* | Published by Revell. |
| 1877 | *Israel's Watchman: A Hebrew-Christian Magazine* | Edersheim was the editor of this magazine. |
| 1878 | *Israel under Samuel, Saul, and David to the Birth of Solomon* | Published by Religious Tract Society. |
| 1882 | *The Laws and Polity of the Jews* | Published by Religious Tract Society. |
| 1883 | *The Life and Times of Jesus the Messiah* | This two-volume work is considered his most important work. It is still in print. |
| 1885 | *The Prophecy and History in Relation to the Messiah: The Warburton Lectures for 1880–1884* | This is a compilation of lectures Edersheim gave during the four-year period from 1880 to 1884 while teaching at Oxford. |
| 1890 | *Tohu-va-Vohu* | This was published posthumously, edited with an extensive memoir by his daughter Ella Edersheim. |

# NOTES

1. Mayhew, "Alfred Edersheim: A Brief Biography," 193–98.

Table 2. Elder James E. Talmage's citations of Edersheim's *Life and Times* in *Jesus the Christ*

| *Jesus the Christ* (1983 ed.) | *Life and Times* | Abbreviated Quotation from *Jesus the Christ*[1] | Reason Edersheim is Cited |
|---|---|---|---|
| **Friend of the Bridegroom**, 160, note 10 | 1:148 | "The institution of 'friends of the bridegroom' prevailed in Judea, but not in Galilee." | An authority on Jewish life and customs |
| **The Targums**, 174, note 4 | 1:10–11 | "It was forbidden . . . to write down a Targum, lest [it] be regarded as of equal authority with the original." | An authority on the Septuagint |
| **Thy Sins Be Forgiven Thee**, 188, note 5 | 1:505–6 | "He presented His person and authority as divine, and He proved it such by the miracle of healing." | An expert on messianic traditions and teachings |
| **The Sabbath Was Made for Man**, 202, note 4 | 1:57–58 | "Ministering to Him was more than ministering in the temple, for He was greater than the temple. If the Pharisees had believed this, they would not have questioned their conduct." | An authority on Jewish life and customs |
| **The Mustard Plant**, 281, note 6 | 1:593 | "A tree, whose wide-spreading branches afforded lodgment to the birds of heaven, was a familiar Old Testament figure for a mighty kingdom that gave shelter to the nations." | An expert on messianic traditions and teachings |
| **Treasure Belonging to the Finder**, 281, note 8 | 1:595–96 | "Some difficulty has been expressed in regard to the morality of such a transaction. In reply it may be observed, that it was, at least, in entire accordance with Jewish law." | An authority on Jewish life and customs |

| Jesus the Christ (1983 ed.) | Life and Times | Abbreviated Quotation from Jesus the Christ[1] | Reason Edersheim is Cited |
|---|---|---|---|
| **Superiority of Our Lord's Parables,** 282, note 9 | 1:580–81 | "[Parables] were almost entirely illustrations of what had been said or taught; while in the case of Christ, they served as the foundation for His teaching." | An authority on Jewish life and customs |
| **The Crucial Nature of the Discourse,** 323, note 11 | 2:36 | "Here then we are at the parting of the two ways. . . . They could not go back to their old past; they must cleave to Him." | A witness of Jesus Christ |
| **The Dogs that Eat,** 341, note 4 | 2:41, fn 5 | "The term means 'little dogs,' or 'house dogs.'" | An expert linguist and translator |
| 347, footnote *p* | 2:79 | Referring to the false doctrine of transmigration or reincarnation of spirits as being "repudiated by the Jews." | A commentator on Jewish doctrine clarifying LDS beliefs |
| **The Feast of Tabernacles,** 391, note 1 | 2:158–60 | "This procession of priests made the circuit of the altar, not only once, but seven times, as if they were again compassing, but now with prayer, the Gentile Jericho." | A commentator on Jewish doctrine clarifying LDS beliefs |
| 395, footnote *l* | 2:138 | "The expression 'if the son of peace be there' is a Hebraism, equivalent to 'if the house be worthy.'" | An expert linguist and translator |
| **Jesus . . . in Bethany,** 415, note 2 | 2:158–60 | "Some writers (e.g. Edersheim) place this incident as having occurred in the course of our Lord's journey to Jerusalem to attend the Feast of Tabernacles" | An authority on Jewish life and customs |

| *Jesus the Christ* (1983 ed.) | *Life and Times* | **Abbreviated Quotation from *Jesus the Christ*[1]** | **Reason Edersheim is Cited** |
|---|---|---|---|
| The Camel, 451, note 7 | 2:343 | "There was a 'common Jewish proverb that a man did not even in his dreams see an elephant pass through the eye of a needle.' " | An authority on Jewish life and customs |
| Undue Concern as to Wages . . . Lord's Service, 452, note 8 | 2:416 | "How utterly mistaken or wrong is the thought that they must necessarily receive more than others, who, seemingly, have done more." | A commentator on Jewish doctrine clarifying LDS beliefs |
| The Temple Treasure, 526, note 8 | 2:387–88 | "Such was the tendency that a law had to be enacted forbidding the gift to the Temple of more than a certain proportion of one's possessions." | An authority on Jewish life and customs |
| Annas . . . Interview with Jesus, 597, note 1 | 2:547–48 | "No figure is better known in contemporary Jewish history than that of Annas." | An authority on Jewish life and customs |
| **Illegalities of the Jewish Trial of Jesus**, 598, note 4 | 1:309 | "The trial and sentence of Jesus in the palace of Caiaphas would have outraged every principle of Jewish criminal law and procedure." | An authority on Jewish life and customs |
| **His Blood Be on Us**, 601, note 5 | 2:578 | "But here, in answer to Pilate's words, came back that deep, hoarse cry: 'His blood be upon us,' and—God help us!—'on our children.' " | A commentator on Jewish doctrine clarifying LDS beliefs |
| **We Have No King but Caesar**, 601, note 6 | 2:581 | "With this cry Judaism was, in the person of its representatives, guilty of denial of God, of blasphemy, of apostasy." | A commentator on Jewish doctrine clarifying LDS beliefs |

| *Jesus the Christ* (1983 ed.) | *Life and Times* | **Abbreviated Quotation from *Jesus the Christ*[1]** | **Reason Edersheim is Cited** |
|---|---|---|---|
| 610, footnote *m* | 2:596 | The clause "if he be the King of Israel" in verse 42 of the common text is admittedly a mistranslation; it should read "He is the King of Israel." | An expert linguist and translator |
| **Christ's Words to the,** 618, note 2 | 2:588 | "The time would come, when the Old Testament curse of barrenness (Hosea 9:14) would be coveted as a blessing." | An authority on Jewish life and customs |
| **Attempts to Discredit,** 648, note 2 | 2:626 | "Not to speak of the many absurdities which this theory involves, it really shifts—if we acquit the disciples of complicity—the fraud upon Christ Himself." | An expert on messianic traditions and teachings |

# Words of Wisdom
# from Edersheim

**(Quotes from his book *Tohu-va-Vohu*)**

This is a short list of the many great quotes that can be found in Edersheim's journal that was published by his daughter Ella after his death. All of these are Edersheim's words. Enjoy! The number at the end of the quote represents the page number in *Tohu-va-Vohu* where the quote is found.

All I really know of God—all I want to know of God—is in Christ. My god is only God in Christ; I know no other, and I do not want to know any other than as there revealed. (20)

―――――

Of all things, the most unlike Christ are His times. (34)

―――――

"Made perfect through suffering." What? Christ or His work? Both. In Christ the subjective and the objective are united. Every step towards His perfecting of salvation, and every progress towards the perfecting of His work was also one towards perfection not His Person but His inner history as the Saviour. Some corresponding outward event in His personal life always accompanies every new stage towards the completion of His work of salvation. (37)

———————

Hold fast by the unity of the Old Testament; not its connection, but its unity. You cannot perceive a mosaic by a little piece of stone. (85)

———————

All prophecy points to the Kingdom of God and to the Messiah as its King. (24)

———————

The New Testament is the organic development and completion of the Old. (26)

———————

In short prophecy cannot be compressed within the four corners of a fact: it is not merely tidings about the future. It is not dead, but instinct with undying life, and that life is divine. There is a moral aspect in prophecy to all generations. Under one aspect of it, it prepares for the future, and this is the predictive element of it. Under its other aspect it teaches lessons of the present to each generation; and this is its moral aspect. (38)

———————

The prophet sees the future in the light of the present, and the present in the light of the future: he wells forth of the waters of God, and he is the man of God. (75)

———————

As when the old world lay submerged in water, the dove carrying the one olive-branch to Noah in the Ark indicated the return of life, which anon would burst forth in a new world, clothed in the green of a fresh spring, so when our Blessed Lord was baptized, and the Holy Ghost in the form of a dove hovered above Him, and proclaimed it into this world of ours: "This is God's beloved Son!" (36–37)

———

ABRAHAM REPRESENTS THE LIFE of faith; Isaac of sonship; Jacob of service; Joseph of rule. (21)

———

THERE IS INFINITE COMFORT and hope even in the fact of being God's creature—the work of His Hand. (1)

———

THERE ARE EVEN GOOD people who suffer from religious or, still worse, from theological dyspepsia. Beware of spiritual biliousness. (3)

———

MAN'S FORGIVENESS IS QUANTITATIVE (how often shall my brother sin against me?). God's forgiveness is qualitative. Man forgives sins; God forgives sin. God's forgiveness both cleans and cleanses; man's can do neither. (10)

———

WITH REVERENCE BE IT said: Our modern theology has almost lost sight of the Father. Our thoughts and our prayers are almost exclusively directed to the Second Person of the Godhead. Yet it is to the Father we are to come through the Son and by the Holy Spirit; and it was the object of the Son to reveal the Father, through the Holy Spirit given unto us. (14)

———

SOMEHOW THE TEMPTER MUST have knowledge of our thoughts, since his temptations are so adapted to them. I do not believe he can search our minds and hearts; but I suppose he can read our actual thinking, which is printed mind, as it were, just as we read the pages of a book. (17)

———

THERE ARE PEOPLE WHO express themselves with such elaborate distinctness as to become at last indistinct, repeating and re-repeating till they succeed in bamboozling themselves and every other person. (21)

---

It is not the sinner, but the sinning, who should tremble. (22)

Thank God for what He reveals and thank God for what He conceals. The faith which follows God into the light is supplemented and completed by that which follows Him in the dark. (22)

---

Even failure becomes precious when the effort has been my own, and not dragged after it by a "because." (25)

---

I am devoutly thankful to God for every evidence in favour of Christianity. Each is a joyous discovery. (28)

---

The world is full of clever people—till it is almost a relief to find a genuine fool. But the worst thing that can happen is when one of these clever people takes to writing about religion. (30)

---

They who would write a Life of Christ aright must themselves also being (in heart and soul) as the Gospels begin—with the angels' song, the worship of the shepherds, and the gifts of the Magi. Or, if they would preach to us from it they must begin like John with this: "Behold the Lamb of God, which taketh away the sin of the world." (30)

---

I have found it most difficult of all simply to submit to God, and not to try to direct my own destinies. (34)

---

If the Epistles of St. Paul were now to appear for the first time, I doubt whether a "religious" publisher would be found to undertake them. Too lax, too doctrinal, too sectarian, too broad, not sensational enough—which shall we say? (41)

---

I AM CONVINCED OF the historical Church; I believe in a national Church; I prefer a liturgical Church and on these grounds I have joined the Church of England. (45)

———

SHUT THE DOOR OF patience upon thy heart, lock it with the key of hope, and in faith hand its keeping over to Him Who is faithful. (47)

———

WE SPEAK OF JOYS departed, never to return. And yet no real joy ever wholly departs, but leaves on the heart a sweet memory of peace. And is not the afterglow more beautiful even than the bright sunlight? Oh, to carry with us an afterflow of life into another world! (49)

———

TRIALS ARE GOD'S VEILED angels to us. (49)

———

WHAT WE CALL DISAPPOINTMENTS are only not God's appointments. (49)

———

MANY CLEVER SAYINGS ARE only logical catchpennies, logical alliterations, which have no more truth—that is, likeness to reality—about them than the alliteration "bow-wow" has to the real bark of a dog. (51)

———

ART, LIKE SCRIPTURE, HAS this for its object: to make us see, through the actual and outward, the spiritual and therefore the truly real. It presents reality, but as that through which we look far away into the ideal, which underlies all, surrounds all, and gives meaning to all. (55)

———

LIVE SLOWLY YOUR LIFE; its joys and its sorrows; its toil and its rest. He must eat slowly that would digest well. (59)

———

MOST OF OUR SORROWS are only such because of our partial knowledge of them. (62)

———————

AS REGARDS THE ETERNAL future, we see it mostly as through the driving rain of our dark winter's day, or through the blinding tears of our heart's agony. (71)

———————

MIRACLES ARE OF CHIEF value as the evidence of a communion between heaven and earth. (71)

———————

WHAT A TERRIBLE PICTURE that of Judas! Once he lost his slender foothold—or rather, it slipped from under him—he fell down, down the eternal abyss. The only hold to which he clung in his fall was that one passion of his soul: covetousness. As he laid hold on it, it gave way with him, and fell with him into fathomless depths. (74)

———————

I FEEL CONVINCED THAT the real root of anti-Semitism is depreciation of the Old Testament. If we have low opinions of the Old Testament we shall come to despise and to hate the Jews, and perhaps not unreasonably so. Love for the Old Testament leads to love for Israel. (78)

———————

THE MIRACULOUS IS ONLY a relative and subjective term. It is the to us unprecedented and uncognisable. . . . I believe in the miraculous—i.e. in the directly Divinely caused, not through a mere fiat, but through a series of natural causation. True—and this is characteristic of the miraculous—we are not able to trace, to perceive, and understand this series of natural causation. But none the less it is there. (82)

———————

WHY ARE PREACHERS IN the habit of asking a series of questions in the pulpit when they immediately add: There are questions which we cannot answer? What can be the use of publicly asking a question which on your own showing you cannot answer? (83)

———————

I BELIEVE IN A personal God; I also believe in a personal Satan. Agnosticism on the latter point seems to me to lay us open to the most serious practical dangers. (85)

I HATE THAT KIND of preaching which pretends to rearing mountains. In reality they are only children making "mud-pies" which they call "mountains." (86)

———————

THE MORE ONE STUDIES ancient, especially Eastern, history in its records, the more is one struck with this as the result of Christianity; the deliverance of the individual—the acknowledgement of individuality, of individual dignity, of moral individuality and individual liberty. . . . Thus, Christianity may well claim to be the founder of modern society and civilization in their ultimate basis and highest aims. (87)

———————

MOST PEOPLE'S MINDS ARE so coarsely constituted that they dwell exclusively upon miracles: they are either their great evidence for Christianity, or else their great objection to it. (97)

———————

BUT THIS COMMUNICATION IS of twofold kind: revelation and miracle—communication by word or by deed: revelation is a miracle by word; miracle is a revelation by deed. (98–99)

———————

IT IS A FALLACY to suppose that age brings wisdom and knowledge. The lapse of time adds nothing to our potentiality, it only develops what is in us. At the age of sixty a man is either a perfect fool, or he ought to have a good deal of sense. (99)

———————

I GLORY IN IT, that there are questions to which no answer can be returned. It shows that there is something above earth and man. (100)

———————

HE IS GREAT WHO is great in small things and small occasions. (104)

---

OUR RELIGIOUS DIFFERENCES MOSTLY spring from what all of us do not know, but pretend to know. (104)

---

JEW AND CHRISTIAN AS I am . . . the benevolent pity over the poor Jew, by those who neither know nor can sympathize with him, my soul abhorreth. (107)

---

SO, THEN IN A sense all books are useful or useless. That, after all, depends on the reader. There are many who "cram," few who read. (112)

---

WE FAIL TO GRASP the sublime thought of the Old Testament. It is: Prophecy fulfilled in Christ. (112)

---

ALL MEN ARE UNDER some influence. The question only is: what that influence is. (122)

---

EVERY MAN HAS HIS own idol, unless he has a God. (125)

---

FAITH IN GOD MAKES us optimists; experience of the world and of men, pessimists. Can we be both at the same time? Yes, by renouncing the world. (126)

# BIBLIOGRAPHY

Backman, Milton V. and Robert L. Millet. "Heavenly Manifestations in the Kirtland Temple (D&C 109, 110, 137)" in Robert L. Millet and Kent P. Jackson, editors, *Studies in Scripture, Vol. 1: The Doctrine and Covenants.* Salt Lake City: Deseret Book, 1989.

Bleefeld, Bradley R. and Shook, Robert L. *Saving the World Entire.* New York: Penguin Group, 1998.

Blaikie, W. G., and H. C. G. Matthew. "John Duncan," *Oxford Dictionary of National Biography.* London: Oxford University Press, 2004, 17:239–40.

Chalybaeus, H. M. *Historical Development of Speculative Philosophy from 1854: Kant to Hegel*, translated by A. Edersheim. Edinburgh: T & T Clark, 1854.

Conference Reports of The Church of Jesus Christ of Latter-day Saints. Salt Lake City: The Church of Jesus Christ of Latter-day Saints, 1898 to present.

Driver, S. R. and Agnew, S. "Alfred Edersheim," *Oxford Dictionary of*

*National Biography*. London: Oxford University Press, 2004. 17:696–97.

Edersheim, Alfred A. *Bible History Old Testament*. Peabody, MA: Hendrickson Publishers, Inc., 1995.

———. *Prophecy and History in Relation to the Messiah: The Warburton Lectures for 1880–1884*. London: Longmans, Green, and Co., 1885.

———. *Sketches of Jewish Social Life: Updated Edition*. Peabody, MA: Hendrickson Publishers, Inc., 1994.

———. *The Life and Times of Jesus the Messiah: New Updated Edition*. Peabody, MA: Hendrickson Publishers, Inc., 2004.

———. *The Jubilee Rhythm of St. Bernard of Clairvaux on the Name of Jesus and Other Hymns*. London: James Nisbet and Company, 1847.

———. *The Temple: Its Ministry and Services*. Grand Rapids, MI: Kregel Publications, 1997.

———. *The Temple: Its Ministry and Services: Updated Edition*. Peabody, MA: Hendrickson Publishers, Inc., 1994.

———. *Tohu-va-Vohu [without form and void]: A collection of fragmentary thoughts and criticisms*. London: Longmans, Green, and Co., 1890.

Fronk, Camille, "The Everlasting Gospel: A Comparison of Dispensations" in *Sperry Symposium: Voices of Old Testament Prophets*. Salt Lake City: Deseret Book, 1997.

Horton, George A., Jr. *The Pearl of Great Price: Revelations from God*. Salt Lake City: Deseret Book, 1989.

Kurts, J. H. *History of the Old Covenant*. Translated by Edersheim. Edinburgh: T & T Clark, 1859.

Ludlow, Daniel H. *A Companion to your Study of Doctrine and Covenants*. Salt Lake City: Deseret Book, 1978.

———. *A Companion to Your Study of the Old Testament*. Salt Lake City: UT: Deseret Book, 1981.

Lund, Gerald N. *A Celebration of Christmas*. Salt Lake City: Deseret Book, 1988.

Madsen, Truman G. *Defender of the Faith: The B. H. Roberts Story*. Salt Lake City: Bookcraft, 1980.

Mayhew, Eugene J. "Alfred Edersheim: A Brief Biography," *Michigan Theological Journal*, 1992, 3:168–99.

McConkie, Bruce R. *Doctrinal New Testament Commentary*. Salt Lake City: Bookcraft, 1973.

———. *The Mortal Messiah*. Vols. 1–4. Salt Lake City: Deseret Book, 1980.

McConkie, Joseph Fielding. *Gospel Symbolism*. Salt Lake City: Deseret Book, 1999.

———. and Millet, Robert L. *Doctrinal Commentary on the Book of Mormon*. Salt Lake City: Deseret Book, 1992.

Millet, Robert L. "The Birth and Childhood of the Messiah (Matthew 1–2; Luke 1–2)," in Kent P. Jackson and Robert L. Millet, editors. *Studies in Scripture*. Vol. 5, *The Gospels*. Salt Lake City: Deseret Book, 1989.

Neander, Johann August. *General History of the Christian Religion and Church*. Translated by Joseph Torrez. Whitefish, MT: Kessinger Publishing Co., 2005.

Parry, Donald W. and Jay A. Parry. *Understanding the Signs of the Times*. Salt Lake City: Deseret Book, 1999.

Roberts, Brigham Henry. *Defense of the Faith and the Saints*. Salt Lake City: Deseret News, 1907.

———. *New Witnesses for God*. Vols. 1–2. Salt Lake City: Deseret News, 1909.

———. *Seventy's Courses in Theology*. Vols. 1–5. Salt Lake City: Deseret News, 1907.

———. *The Mormon Doctrine of Deity*. Salt Lake City: Deseret News, 1903.

—. *The Truth, The Way, The Life.* Edited by John W. Welch. Provo, UT: BYU Studies, 1996.

Smart, William B. *Messages for a Happier Life: Inspiring Essays from the Church News.* Salt Lake City: Deseret Book, 1989.

Smith, Joseph Fielding. *The Restoration of All Things.* Salt Lake City: Deseret Book, 1945.

—. *Church History and Modern Revelation.* Salt Lake City: Deseret Book, 1946.

Springhall, J. "Sir George Williams," *Oxford Dictionary of National Biography.* London: Oxford University Press, 2004. 59:192–93.

Talmage, James E. *Jesus the Christ: A Study of the Messiah and His Mission according to Holy Scriptures both Ancient and Modern.* Salt Lake City: Deseret Book, 1976.

—. *Jesus the Christ.* Salt Lake City: Deseret Book, 1983.

# About the Author

Marianna Edwards Richardson enjoys studying and reading about a variety of topics. She received a bachelor of arts degree from Brigham Young University in English literature, with a minor in art history. She also earned a master's degree from Johns Hopkins University in special education and a doctorate in education from Seattle Pacific University in curriculum and development. She is the assistant to the editor of the American Counseling Association journal *Counseling and Values*. She has presented papers internationally on such subjects as the life and times of Alfred Edersheim, achievement motivation in education, and the teaching of moral behavior to children.

The most important work she does is to care for her large family. She has been married to Dr. Stephen D. Richardson for over thirty years, and they have twelve wonderful children and six grandchildren (with more on the way). Marianna and Steve currently live in Redmond, Washington.